# The Festivals of Canada

## ARNOLD EDINBOROUGH

LESTER
&ORPEN
DENNYS
PUBLISHERS

**Canadian Cataloging in Publication Data**

Main entry under title:
The Festivals of Canada

ISBN 0-919630-33-2

1. Theater – Canada – Pictorial works.
2. Theater – Canada – History.   3. Centers for
the performing arts – Canada – Pictorial works.
4. Centers for the performing arts – Canada –
History.   5. Drama festivals.   I. Edinborough,
Arnold, 1922-

PN2304.F47     792´.0971     C80-094775-4

Design:  Jack Steiner Graphic Design
Photo Research:  Viki Colledge
Production:  Paula Chabanais

Printed and bound in Canada for

Lester & Orpen Dennys Ltd.
78 Sullivan Street
Toronto, Ontario M5T 1C1

Also by Arnold Edinborough
One Church, Two Nations
Some Camel, Some Needle
The Enduring Word (*edited*)

For Kip, Aly and Sarah
– who were often there too.

11

*The
Guelph
Spring
Festival*

35

*The
Stratford
Festival*

91

*The
Shaw
Festival*

133

157

181

201

*The Charlottetown Festival*

*The National Arts Centre Festival*

*Festival Lennoxville*

*The Banff Festival of the Arts*

# INTRODUCTION

Of course, there have been festivals of drama and music for a long time. The Greeks had festivals of plays which must have demanded the uttermost from their audiences, sitting for hours under the Mediterranean sun. The Welsh have had music festivals since before the year 1000 A.D.; they were called *eisteddfodau*, which means "sittings", and sittings indeed they were, doubtless in the rain, while angry bards struggled to out-sneer each other. There has long been a festival at Bayreuth, to the greater glory of Richard Wagner, and for a shorter time a festival at Salzburg, to the even greater glory of Mozart. Edinburgh has a festival and so has Bath; the civilized world is alive with festivals, some of which are notably more festive than others.

But Canada? The book which follows is splendid evidence of how far we have come in the matter of festivals in a little more than a quarter of a century. When I was a youth – and a born festival-goer if ever there was one – the festivals were all abroad, and had the enchantment of what is far away. I went to Stratford-on-Avon several times, and gobbled Shakespeare at six evening and two matinée performances; I went to Malvern, and saw a week of plays that covered four hundred years of English drama, beginning with *Ralph Roister Doister* (a rib-binder dating from about 1550, and notable for one of Ralph Richardson's early performances as Mathew Merrygreeke) and finishing with Shaw's latest, *Too True to Be Good*. But there was nowhere to go in Canada. Lucky young people in our time, who can stay in their own country and see Shakespeare better done than at the parent Stratford, and an extraordinary range of opera, as well as splendid music, much of which is being presented for the first time!

It is one of the boasts of our Stratford that playgoers who began to go there as schoolchildren at special matinées, now come and bring their children. If they buy their tickets wisely, students can see, in the course of a few years, the whole Shakespeare canon played as well as they could see it anywhere in the world, including such rarities as *Pericles*, *Titus Andronicus* and *Timon of Athens*, which used to be dismissed, when I was at university, as lesser plays, but which prove to have splendid qualities that reveal themselves in sympathetic production.

At many Canadian festivals it has been my privilege to be in the same audience as the author of this book, an old friend and one of the greatest Enjoyers I have ever had the luck to know. It is part of the charm of festivals that people go to them in order to enjoy themselves, and the atmosphere of a festival audience is agreeably different from that which envelops a winter audience, sometimes like a wet old woolly blanket. The austerest of intellectuals relax a little at a summer arts festival, not because they have left their critical principles at home – the festival standards of performance in drama, opera and music are fully as exacting as those of winter performances – but because there is something about summer which is friendly to art. Maybe it is because we do not have to attend cumbered with overcoats, fur caps and galoshes, which must be left in the *garderobes* and expensively ransomed when the show is over. Maybe it is because we have dined or picnicked with unusual splendour beforehand (though the rumour that first-night audiences are full of drunks is a vile *canard* circulated by nervous performers). Maybe it is because the Greeks were right when, 2500 years ago, they held their festivals in fine weather.

Whatever the cause, the festivals are lively affairs in Canada, and we are rightly proud of them. This book supports and enlarges that pride, and I am happy to ring the bell, or shoot off the gun, that introduces Arnold Edinborough's personal performance.

July 26, 1980
and the 124th anniversary of
the birth of Bernard Shaw,
tutelary spirit of one of
our festivals.

ROBERTSON DAVIES

# The Festivals of Canada

_The Guelph Spring Festival_

THE GUELPH SPRING FESTIVAL _is the one that comes before the summer dares and fills the city's halls with beauty. A month before Stratford and Shaw, two months before Lennoxville, Ottawa and Charlottetown and three before Banff, it is the nation's curtain-raiser in every sense of that word, for it is short, concentrated and whets the musical and dramatic appetite for what will follow._

_It comes at just the right time. Winter is long drawn out even in central Canada and ends, not in a blaze of pink blossom, blue skies and yellow daffodils as it does in Europe, but in stubborn piles of dirty snow, flash storms of icy rain, and left-over heaps of semi-composted autumn leaves. Spirits are low in our Ontario March, and their rise in April is slow and fluctuating. To go to the Guelph Festival in April is to put winter definitively behind and summer equally definitively before._

Not that its founders necessarily had such climatic considerations in mind. For them, all of them academics at the University of Guelph, it was the most opportune time. Through the winter, in hours spared from the lecture and committee room, they could plan the season, organize the publicity and administer the box office. By the end of March, lectures are over and examinations set. With papers marked in early April, May is always a recreative month. The major halls of the university are free of normal classes, but still operating; the university population is still in the city with relatively little to do. The community is ready for such an occasion as the Festival provides.

The community – that's the key word. Guelph is a community festival. It welcomes visitors from Toronto and other cities of the populous Ontario south-west, but the programme is aimed at the citizens of Guelph and the academic entity which has been in their midst for over a century. In their midst, because only recently has the academic component become a university. For almost the first century of its existence, what is now the University of Guelph was then three colleges: the Ontario Agricultural College, the Ontario Veterinary College and the Macdonald Institute of Home Economics, all of which directly served the rich farming area in which Guelph sits.

A well-to-do town, Guelph shows its historic wealth in a number of fine old limestone houses and several equally fine stone churches, one of which, the Church of Our Lady, dominates the city, its twin towers rising on the highest piece of ground for miles around. Seat of county government, site of the province's only agricultural and veterinary colleges, market-town for the rich land of Wellington County, Guelph was also the home-town of Edward Johnson, one of the most distinguished tenors of this century, who later became the general manager of the Metropolitan Opera in New York. In the words of Murdo MacKinnon, the prime mover and perennial president of the Guelph Festival, Edward Johnson "was...a one-man cultural revolution [who] not only dreamed of making Guelph a musical city but took vigorous action to make it happen. He sponsored a Spring Festival of Music, he gave money for music scholarships, he gave concerts himself in Guelph, he visited the schools, he encouraged great performers to come to Guelph."

He was also chairman of the Board of the Royal Conservatory in Toronto and its Opera School. Nicholas Goldschmidt, one of the early directors of the school, says that Johnson "delighted the young aspiring singers with his inimitable charm and his words of encouragement....His was an inspirational face that radiated from his professional experiences and his glorious voice. Those who knew him admired his faith in Canadian talent and his determination to foster it."

Those who admired him did more. The members of the Guelph Rotary Club, of which Johnson was an honorary member during his retirement, put up the money for the Edward Johnson Foundation, dedicated to his memory and its perpetuation in musical terms. That Foundation, through the energy of Murdo MacKinnon and the musical talents of Nicholas Goldschmidt (by then a professor of music within the university) was the seed from which the Guelph Festival sprang, and it is the Foundation which is still the sponsor of the Festival.

There were two dominant ideas in the evolution of the Festival. Both were statements by Johnson himself:

...of all the arts that serve mankind, none is more powerful nor more universal than music....We hold to the pattern of the past while formulating a design for the future; we work with but a single purpose: to keep alive the torch that in due time we may pass it on to our successors, undiminished in beauty and strength.

The other was even more to the Festival's point:

Make no small plans for they have no power to excite the minds and hearts of men.

The MacKinnon–Goldschmidt team was an excellent combination to turn these large ideas into reality. MacKinnon had founded Wellington College, the arts college which came into being in the university expansion of the mid-sixties and which made it possible for the existing professional colleges in Guelph to come together as a true university. Goldschmidt, a mid-thirties refugee from Europe, had been an original faculty member of the Opera School at the University of Toronto, then artistic director of the highly ambitious International Festival in Vancouver, which after ten years of brilliance foundered from financial difficulties at a time when subsidization of the arts was still unusual in Canada. He had then coordinated all the musical activities of Canada's Centennial Year in 1967 and moved to the faculty at Guelph when the Centennial was over.

MacKinnon knew almost everybody in Guelph; Goldschmidt knew almost everybody in the world of music, both in Canada and abroad.

There was one big drawback: there was no concert hall in Guelph. Even War Memorial Hall in the university was quite small and had been designed for lectures, convocations and other university events; it would only do for solo recitals and small orchestras. But the churches, especially the Roman Catholic Church of Our Lady and St. George's Anglican Church, were good spaces with good acoustics. They also had large congregations which might serve as a target audience, particularly if the offerings therein were choral. (Parents, cousins, uncles and aunts are easy ticket sales for choral society members.)

So the programme for the first Guelph Festival in 1968 was worked out, with an initial lecture on Edward Johnson by the assistant manager of the Metropolitan Opera, Francis Robinson, and the archivist Mary Ellis Peltz, and an exhibition of Johnson memorabilia put together by Molly Middleton of the University of Guelph and mounted by William Lord, then the chief scenic designer of the Canadian Opera Company. The opening concert, in St. George's Anglican Church, consisted of music by Bach, Handel and Mozart, performed by the organist of St. George's, Ralph Kidd; his choir; a pick-up local orchestra; and, as soprano soloist, Eleanor Calbes, a protégée of Goldschmidt. (Her training at the Royal Conservatory in Toronto had been financed by scholarships for which she had auditioned after attracting Goldschmidt's notice at the Vancouver International Festival six years earlier.)

The following evening, in the Church of Our Lady, a concert of religious music was sung by the Festival Singers of Canada under Elmer Iseler, then just beginning to enjoy an international reputation after recording music by Stravinsky under Stravinsky's own enthusiastic direction.

In the next two weeks came a concert in Memorial Hall by soprano Lois Marshall, a showcase of works by University of Toronto music students and a final concert with the

Guelph Light Opera Company and Oratorio Chorus conducted by Charles Wilson, who was himself commissioned to compose a piece for the occasion, and who chose to set to music a poem by a fellow faculty member and award-winning poet, Douglas Jones.

For theatre people, there were five performances by Montreal's Instant Theatre, one of whose plays was an original Canadian comedy, Kay Hill's *Cobbler Stick to thy Last*.

This first festival thus carried on the spirit of the Centennial in giving Canadians the spotlight as both composers and performers. It also involved the musicians in the city and in the faculty of music at the university. But it went out to the community as well, in its tribute to Edward Johnson, whose eight years of retirement in Guelph before his death in 1959 had made him a familiar figure as well as a famous one.

To underline the community's role even further, there was on the second weekend of the three-weekend festival a "mammoth parade with floats and seven bands", walking and running road races, an imported town fool (Kim Voikis from Vancouver), a variety show, a jazz performance in the main town square and – through Operation Aladdin – illuminations of Guelph's historic buildings by Ontario Hydro.

Good performances of music by old masters, together with premières of music by new composers; classical concerts and community involvement; the celebration of Guelph's architectural beauty and open hospitality for out-of-town visitors, made that first festival a great artistic success – and the box-office was sufficient to keep the Foundation solvent, after donations from local business and grants from the provincial and federal councils were added in.

Having put their hands to the festival plough (to use a metaphor not unusual in the University of Guelph), the organizers were now committed to carrying on and cultivating yearly the area they had marked out for themselves. For the next two years, they concentrated on themes. As it was the basis for their initial success, Arts in Religion was the theme for 1969, with a church opera by Benjamin Britten, *The Prodigal Son*, four miracle plays done by the University of Toronto's amateur medieval drama group, Poculi Ludique Societas, and an exhibition of religious art from Quebec. In 1970, the bi-centennial of Beethoven's birth, the theme was Beethoven: The Man and his Time, which opened with the Oratorio Chorus singing Beethoven's *Mass in C* in the Church of Our Lady and continued with the National Arts Centre orchestra under Karl Münchinger, playing the *Ritter* ballet music and the *Second Symphony*. But by now it was clear that the festival, though still very much a Guelph affair (65% of tickets were, and still are, bought in Guelph), had become a festival of national importance and international standing. Jon Vickers had given a concert in 1969; Karl Münchinger had conducted the NAC orchestra in 1970 and Beverly Sills was contracted for 1971.

Themes can be limiting and the programming at Guelph was more at home with a multiple mix than a rigid theme. How could commissioned works by Canadian composers which suited the funding agencies, church operas by Benjamin Britten which suited the choral groups and the church spaces, solo recitals by great artists which suited Memorial Hall and art exhibitions which suited the residents be put together in a theme? So the programme for 1971 said: "We have decided that for 1971 and future years our theme will be simply our title 'Guelph Spring Festival.'"

And what has been the result?

First, a flowering of contemporary Canadian music unmatched in any other centre in the country. In the thirteen years that the Edward Johnson Foundation has sponsored the Guelph Festival, it has commissioned works by Norma Beecroft, Harry Somers, André Prévost, Godfrey Ridout, Charles Wilson, Oskar Morawetz, Clermont Pépin, Gary Hayes, Derek Holman and George Fiala, among others. It has also performed works by a dozen other Canadian composers, often in conjunction with the Canadian Broadcasting Corporation so that the performance heard in Guelph one evening is heard across Canada shortly after. As Keith MacMillan, former director of the Canadian Music Centre, remembered in 1974: "The positive achievements of the Festival have been notable, especially in its stimulus to Canadian music."

Second, a balance between the old reliables – Mozart, Haydn, Beethoven, Schubert and so on – and the new ones. A showcase concert in 1968 had not only Dowland and Schubert but also Villa-Lobos and Hindemith; a concert by the Festival Singers in 1971 had Harry Somers' *Gloria*, Rachmaninoff's *Three Anthems*, Gabrieli's *Jubilate Deo* and Healey Willan's *Gloria Deo Per Immensa Saecula*. In 1975 the Tokyo String Quartet played Berg as well as Brahms, and in 1977 the Toronto Brass Quintet played Bach and Messiaen.

One of the most extraordinary and memorable evenings for music in the whole decade was at Guelph on May 8, 1976. On that evening in War Memorial Hall, Krzysztof Penderecki directed a concert of his own works. Acknowledged as one of the world's leading contemporary composers, he had yet accepted Nicholas Goldschmidt's invitation with alacrity, especially when Goldschmidt said he should choose whatever he wanted to present and the Guelph Festival would find him the performers.

Penderecki chose a cello sonata, three choral works, a string quartet and a percussion piece. Indicative of both Goldschmidt's persuasiveness and Guelph's standing in the musical world, the following were contracted to perform the concert: Mary Morrison, soprano; Robert Aitken, flute; the Festival Singers; the Nexus Percussion Ensemble; the Orford String Quartet and Gisela Depkat, cello.

That concert, of fiendish difficulty and haunting quality, stirred everyone to a standing ovation and led critics in the continental press to burble their praise. Penderecki was ecstatic, rushing down the aisle of War Memorial Hall to embrace Elmer Iseler of the Festival Singers, whose members had produced unbelievable sounds with precision and joy.

Penderecki was not the first international superstar at Guelph. Yehudi Menuhin had preceded him in 1974. His participation was a typical result of Goldschmidt's methods. Just over a year before, Menuhin was playing with the Toronto Symphony. During his stay, Goldschmidt, an old friend, invited him to dinner after his daytime rehearsal. Would he come to the Guelph Festival, Goldschmidt wanted to know. Well, said Menuhin, he was always so booked up. Was he, in fact, asked Goldschmidt, booked for April 27, 1974. No, said Menuhin, he was, in fact, not. Then come.

It was not as easy as all that, said Menuhin. What would he play? He wanted something new and vibrant for such an occasion and very few modern composers were interested in solo violin. The answer to that was easy: Goldschmidt would commission something. Had Menuhin ever heard Harry Somers' music? No, he had not. So Goldschmidt asked Harry Somers to come over with a tape of some of his work. Menuhin listened, then said, "Will you commission him or shall I?"

So *Music for Solo Violin* was, as the manuscript in Somers' precise hand states at the top, "commissioned by Yehudi Menuhin with the assistance of the Canada Council for the première at the Guelph Spring Festival 1974." Underneath is the superscription: "To Nickie – without whose suggestion, diplomacy, and co-ordinating ability this work would not exist. Many thanks!! Harry."

Thus modern music and Canadian music have been two of the main strands in the musical web that is annually woven at Guelph. Another has been church opera – not so strange, of course, when one remembers that church spaces provide the best acoustic settings with the maximum number of seats in the city. After beginning with Britten's *The Prodigal Son* in 1969, the festival then produced his *The Burning Fiery Furnace* (1971) and *Noyes Fludde* (1972), all in the Church of Our Lady.

The success of these productions, which also underlined the festival's connection with Edward Johnson and the Metropolitan Opera, encouraged the organizers to mount chamber operas in a school auditorium. Now, a school auditorium is not the place for opera; the wings and backstage facilities for scene-shifting, the cleared open area in front of the stage which has to do duty as an orchestra pit, the overall atmosphere of chalkdust and gym shoes, are enough to put even amateurs off. For professionals, especially when converted classrooms serve as dressing-rooms, a high-school auditorium is about the worst place in the world.

So who turned up in 1974 to sing the chorus in Britten's *Rape of Lucretia*? Jon Vickers, the same Vickers who will not go near the professional opera companies in Toronto, but who recognizes the standard, the panache, the outright quality of Guelph, and who found in those same weeks he was there not only Yehudi Menuhin, but also Maureen Forrester, Maria Pellegrini, Louis Quilico, Lois Marshall and the Mendelssohn Choir.

And in 1979, Gian Carlo Menotti, whose opera *The Consul* had been put on in 1973, was commissioned to write a special opera for the International Year of the Child. Based on a fairy tale, *Chip and his Dog* was performed by the Canadian Children's Opera Chorus to great acclaim from the audience and to the immense satisfaction of Menotti, who helped to prepare the opera performance before leaving to see Beverly Sills in the world première of his other new opera of the year, *Juana la Loca*, at the San Diego Opera.

This was the second opera the Guelph Festival had commissioned. In 1977, Derek Healey had been asked to write the music for a libretto by Norman Newton entitled *Seabird Island*. Healey is essentially a church musician and Newton a Canadian Broadcasting Corporation producer. Between them they produced perhaps the only major flop the Guelph Festival has ever had. But Guelph was at least ready to do it. And outside of Guelph, no one in Canada has commissioned an opera in the past decade.

Theatre is less important to the Guelph Festival. It is, after all, a kind of *maggio musicale* – a spring festival of music. And yet, in the same year that *Seabird Island* was lost in a sea of noise, Siobhan McKenna was performing in the world première of *Memoir*, an original play by a Calgary writer, John Murrell. The writing of *Memoir* was witty, lyrical and eccentric to the point of craziness. Based on the memoirs of Sarah Bernhardt, the play was a triumph and has since made a comfortable transition to both London and New York.

In thirteen short years, then, the Guelph Spring Festival has achieved a remarkable status in the international music community. It has honoured, on special occasions and in different media, such diverse musicians as Penderecki, Menuhin, Beethoven and its prime begetter, Edward Johnson. It has commissioned over twenty new works from Canadian composers and given a warm and welcoming platform to Jon Vickers, Sir Peter Pears, Martina Arroyo and Jan Peerce.

In its ninth season, it brought the Juilliard String Quartet in to play all the Bartók quartets in two memorable evenings, and in 1978 it devoted three separate concerts to Schubert – with the Orford String Quartet, the piano duo of Victor Bouchard and Renée Morisset and a host of singers led by Peter Pears.

In 1980, the 100th anniversary of the birth of Healey Willan – perhaps Canada's best-known composer, certainly of sacred music – the opening concert was devoted to him, with Lorand Fenyves playing his *Violin Sonata No. 1*, Lois Marshall singing a selection of his songs and the Elmer Iseler Singers some of his choral works. As a finale, Harry Somers' new work, specially commissioned in tribute to Healey Willan, was performed by the whole group plus the Stratford Ensemble.

From outside came Nicolai Gedda to fill Memorial Hall with gorgeous tenor sound, and the Kreutzberger String Quartet of Berlin to pay tribute to Ernst Křenek, an Austrian composer celebrating his 80th birthday.

In St. Joseph's Church, Berlioz's *L'Enfance du Christ* was presented with twenty animated life-size figures by puppeteers Felix Mirbt and Carolyn Davis. The production also included a distinguished group of Canadian singers, the Kitchener-Waterloo Symphony, the Kitchener Bach Choir and the Angel Choir of local children.

Innovation, high standards, remarkable diversity of programming and constant local involvement: these have been, and will continue to be, the solid base on which the Guelph Spring Festival's reputation is built. The same people who invented it have brought it, by such methods, from a budget of $27,000 to $270,000, from a local celebration to a national event. "But", says Murdo MacKinnon, "the Guelph Festival is not a tourist attraction, although we welcome guests from Toronto and other centres. It is an attempt by the university and the citizens of Guelph to mount as good a two weeks of music and entertainment as they can, principally for their own enjoyment. We have, of course, never compromised with standards, but then a university shouldn't. It should set them."

In the elegant old limestone city of Guelph, with its Church of Our Lady sitting massively on the hill and the Speed and Eramosa rivers running quietly through the valley below, the Guelph Festival has done just that – set standards by which any other music festival in the country has to be judged. But it has done more. It has kept the rural atmosphere of Guelph, and its natural ease of hospitality which makes the Festival indeed a tonic for the spring.

The Guelph Spring Festival

1    *Puppeteer Felix Mirbt operating one of the sculptural shapes he helped design for Berlioz's oratorio* **L'Enfance du Christ**, *1980*

1    **L'Enfance du Christ** *at Guelph was a fascinating experiment using larger-than-life sculpted figures designed by Carolyn Davis and Felix Mirbt*

2    *Conductor Nicholas Goldschmidt rehearsing the Kitchener Bach Choir, the Victor Martens Chamber Singers, the Kitchener-Waterloo Symphony, an Angel Chorus of local children and soloists Gary Relyea, Claude Corbeil, Paul Trépanier*

3

4

**3** *Design sketch by William Lord for the Chester miracle play* **Noyes Fludde**. *Set to music by Benjamin Britten, 1972*

**4** *Allan Monk as Noah, Patricia Rideout as his wife, together with their family both human and animal*

1    *Maureen Forrester as the Witch with Kathy Terrell as Hansel and Eleanor Calbes as Gretel. A 1979 production of* **Hansel and Gretel**, *music by Engelbert Humperdinck*

2    *A scene from* **Inook and the Sun** *by Henry Beissel, music by Georgi Nachoff. A Young People's Theatre presentation in 1975*

3 **The Beggar's Opera** by Benjamin Britten presented in 1976. Judith Forst as Polly Peachum, Barbara Carter as Lucy Lockit and Emile Belcourt as Macheath

4 *In another scene from the same production Emile Belcourt adjusts the garter of Dolly Trull sung by Susan Gudgeon*

5 **The Prodigal Son**, *Benjamin Britten's first major work to be presented by the Festival, with Peter van Ginkel, Garnet Brooks and John Arab, 1969*

1    *Garnet Brooks as the Shaman,*
*Roxolana Roslak as the Indian*
*Princess in* Seabird Island *by Derek*
*Healey and Norman Newton*

2    *Handel's oratorio* Acis and
Galatea, *based on a classical tale*
*from Ovid's* Metamorphoses, *with*
*Don McManus, Eleanor Calbes and*
*Sheila Barnes, 1975*

3    *The Festival Singers as the*
*chorus in* Acis and Galatea, *visible*
*through the scrim*

4    **Memoir**, *an original play by
John Murrell based on the memoirs
of Sarah Bernhardt, 1977. Siobhan
McKenna as La Divine Sarah,
Gerard Parkes as Georges Pitou*

1    *Two principal dancers of Les
Grands Ballets Canadiens show
their skill in* **After Eden** *during their
1978 visit to the Festival*

**2** *Les Grands Ballets Canadiens in* **Tam Ti Delam**, *choreographed by Brian MacDonald with music by Gilles Vigneault, 1978*

**3** *The Canadian Mime Theatre, Canada's first professional mime theatre, performing at Guelph, 1977*

1     *The Nexus Percussion Ensemble playing a range of instruments from traditional drums to their own inventions, 1976*

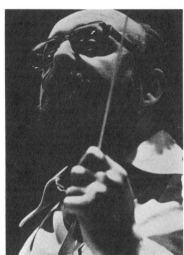

**2**    *The Guelph Concert Singers
rehearsing under their conductor
Dr Charles Wilson in the Church of
Our Lady, 1972*

**3**    *The passion of Penderecki is
clear in this picture of him rehearsing for an evening of music at the
Festival*

1    *Yehudi Menuhin not only came to Guelph but also commissioned Harry Somers to write a piece for solo violin performed in 1974. In this picture Menuhin is with his sister Hepzibah*

**2**    *The twin-towered Catholic Church of Our Lady is Guelph's most dominant and beautiful landmark*

# The Stratford Festival

STRATFORD, ONTARIO, *has the biggest summer festival – and the oldest – in Canada. Between 1970 and 1980 over five million people saw the productions there, choosing from a hundred different shows in three different theatres – a long way from the original season in 1953, when fewer than 70,000 people chose between two shows. The season then ran for six weeks with 42 performances.*

*Before 1953, the Stratford Festival was merely a recurring fantasy in the mind of one man, Tom Patterson, who thought that a town called Stratford, which had a street called Romeo and a neighbouring village called Shakespeare, should do more about its English roots than mere nomenclature. Knowing nothing of theatre, he talked to people who did. Both Dora Mavor Moore, the grand old lady of Canadian theatre even then, and Robertson Davies, a playwright who had been with* the Old Vic Company in England in the late thirties, advised him to contact Tyrone Guthrie. Guthrie was an innovator, a man who liked challenges, and he was known to both of them. Moreover, he had experimented with an open, non-proscenium stage at the Edinburgh Festival in 1948, and had said to the Shakespeare Stage Society in 1952:

> There will be no drastic improvement in staging Shakespeare until there is a return to certain basic conditions of the Shakespeare stage. There is no need for an exact replica of the Globe Theatre but it is essential to make the contact between the players and audience as intimate as possible.

So when Guthrie was approached by Dora Mavor Moore his reply was, from such an international personality, encouraging:

> I am intensely interested to produce Shakespeare on a stage which might reproduce the actor-audience relation for which he wrote. . . . I assume that at Stratford, Ont., the stage and auditorium are still to be made. And, if I could influence their design, I will be very happy to do so.

Patterson phoned him immediately and asked him to come to Stratford to expound his ideas to the planning committee. The committee was impressed by his enthusiasm and clear objective; he was impressed by what he called "a pioneering venture of a gallant and unselfish kind".

Given the go-ahead, Guthrie recruited Tanya Moiseiwitsch to design the stage, and Alec Guinness and Irene Worth to be the two leading actors of the first season.

The story of the building of the stage, and the raising of the money to pay for it as well as for the huge canvas tent to cover it, is now part of Canadian theatre history, well documented in several books, of which Guthrie's own *A Life in the Theatre* is the most candid and Robertson Davies' *Renown at Stratford* the most amusing.

At one leap, Stratford, a small, somewhat depressed repair centre for the Canadian National Railway, became the major theatrical centre in the country.

It has never let the title go since. Alec Guinness and Irene Worth came from England to play *Richard III* and *All's Well That Ends Well* in that tent, and on that extraordinary stage; James Mason came from Hollywood to play Angelo in *Measure for Measure*; Frederick Valk, an immensely powerful actor, came from Europe to play Shylock in *The Merchant of Venice*; and Douglas Campbell, Tony van Bridge, Donald Davis, Douglas Rain, William Hutt, Bruno Gerussi, Eleanor Stuart and Frances Hyland came from various theatrical enterprises across Canada.

The tent was insufferably hot on humid summer days; it produced a deafening *continuo* to the actors' speeches when that humidity was broken with a thunderstorm. Yet, for four years, with lengthening seasons and increasing audiences, it was ritually raised every June and folded away each August, many Stratfordians turning out to watch that remarkable tent-man, Skip Manley, supervise the job. Best show of the season, some Stratfordians unworthily thought.

But in 1956 the great canvas tent was folded for the last time. In 1957 a soaring beautiful building, a carousel in brick and wood and glass, finally gave the stage a still festive but permanent home, its 425-ton roof topped off with a great white coronet from which the festival flag triumphantly flew.

There are 2262 seats in the Festival Theatre – 1404 on the main floor and 858 in the balcony. The seats are ranged in a 220° arc around the stage, and no member of the audience is more than 65 feet away.

The peak of the hexagonal roof is directly above the central pillar of the stage balcony. To go to the theatre at Stratford, therefore, is to enter into a total theatrical environment. Players may come down the aisles, up through two tunnels beneath the audience, from either side of the stage, from the centre back, onto the balcony above or up from a trapdoor below.

Such a setting makes the swirl of Shakespeare's histories particularly exciting, as it does all battle scenes. Guthrie set the pattern with *Richard III* in that first season in 1953 and before the decade was out it was followed by *Henry IV: Part I*, *Henry V* and *King John*, as well as *Hamlet*, *Othello* and *Julius Caesar*, all of which have military scenes.

But apart from bringing the swirl of battle so close (one sword fight inadvertently came near to cropping the nose of the Governor General, Vincent Massey, on one robustious opening night), the intimacy of the theatre can be used for equally involving emotional turmoil, whether it be Julie Harris as a truly remarkable Juliet or Frances Hyland as a crushingly destroyed Desdemona.

Whatever it does, though, it calls for skilled acting and even more skilled directing. As Michael Langham (who succeeded Guthrie as artistic director in 1956) says: "On the picture frame or 'operatic' stage the actors must needs play to the audience and only *pretend* to play to each other, while on the open stage their bond of relationship is direct, true and complete, and serves to pull the audience deeply into the experience of the play." Yet while actors thus are being naturalistic and intense, their backs may well be to some part of the audience. Unskilled directors are apt to invent business and send actors on stage-encircling promenades to alleviate this. Such movement *can* put a stop to the intimacy and naturalness, because it is seen to be a stage trick. Pretend stage movement is no better than pretend stage involvement. And a good many directors, from both Canada and elsewhere, have produced some less than engrossing work at Stratford. Other directors have learned the stage well, exploited its unusual opportunities and done work which has made Stratford the international phenomenon that it is. Three of these became artistic directors: Michael Langham, Jean Gascon and Robin Phillips.

Langham was brought to Stratford by Guthrie in 1955 to direct *Julius Caesar*, an apprentice piece which did not foreshadow Langham's future greatness at Stratford except in two scenes: one in which Cinna the poet was totally dismembered on stage and vanished into fragments before our eyes, and the other at the end of the play when all had gone but Octavius Caesar and Mark Antony, prefiguring their later clash – for chaos, Langham showed us, breeds chaos. That sensitivity to both the text and the stage made Langham's tenure as artistic director an exciting and often overwhelming affair. In *Henry V*, for example, all the French court were played by Francophone actors from Quebec, including the ravishing Ginette Letondal as Katherine, and, happy choice, Jean Gascon as the constable. And *Romeo and Juliet* starred Julie Harris as a Juliet of fragile beauty and enormous emotional power. That power was especially demonstrated when, in the middle of the ball, Romeo declared his love. The two were illuminated in a blinding white light, with the whole of the rest of the cast frozen in mid-gesture.

Langham's triumph though, and arguably the best production ever on the Stratford stage, was that little-played early comedy *Love's Labour's Lost*. One would not expect this because *Love's Labour's Lost* is very much a private Elizabethan joke rather than a modern comedy. In it Shakespeare satirizes the ink-horn terms of Tudor schoolmasters, the flatulent pseudo-elegance of Euphuism and the affected foreign gestures used by vapid courtiers. In addition to this detailed stylistic satire, the play is also a general satire on romantic comedy and the artificiality of Tudor court life.

The temptation, therefore, is to play tricks with the text and to make the actors farcical to get a modern laugh at Shakespeare's ancient expense. It is to the eternal credit of Michael Langham that he didn't do this. He went on the assumption that a line which has a witty point can be so spoken that it will seem witty even if the allusion is not quite clear. In this he was ably abetted by his actors, all of whom entered into the frothy spirit of the piece.

They were led by Paul Scofield as Armado, whose wonderfully articulated and elegantly mannered performance was a delight, to both the eye and the ear. But no less good was Zoë Caldwell as Rosaline, whose pertness, vivacity and blissful clarity made the audience watch her, and her alone, whenever she was on even a crowded stage.

Rosaline's foil, Berowne (played by John Colicos), was a match for her, even if he did occasionally race his speech. Douglas Rain, in dove-grey foppery, was an amazing bag of courtly tricks – in both voice and gesture. And as the King of Navarre, the cranky instigator of the phoney study period, Leo Ciceri was equally clear and convincing.

The farcical relief provided by Shakespeare himself in the form of Costard, Holofernes and Sir Nathaniel was also highly enjoyable, but still within the limits of the delicate framework on which this play rests. Eric Christmas made marvellous play with the two words "remuneration" and "guerdon". Holofernes was obviously Jack Creley's true *métier* and his agile footwork, his ridiculous makeup and his range of vocal inflection made him understandable even to a modern audience, as well as to Sir Nathaniel, lugubriously but merrily played by William Needles.

Led by Joy Parker as the Princess of France, all the ladies were pleasant to look at and vivacious, whether it was the vivacity of hoydenism in Kate Reid's Jaquenetta or the more refined version of Maria (Mary Anderson) and Katharine (Michael Learned).

But none of this could have come off, nor could the cast have done so well, had not Mr. Langham carefully, subtly, patiently constructed the nice balance of the whole production, a balance which poised itself right to the last scene of the play, which is often spoiled by heavy-handedness.

In Mr. Langham's production the Masque of the Nine Worthies had swollen into riotous horseplay when the messenger announced the death of the Tudor Princess' father. Immediately the quips and quiddities, the low clowning and the rarefied artificiality disappeared, and careless youth must face responsibilities devolving from an older generation's death – a dangerous and sudden transition. Langham did it by staging the whole farewell against the background of the two songs – the cuckoo song which gently derides the whole charade which has gone before and the winter one, setting the proper chilling mood for facing the cold facts of life. Consummately timed, the ending was thus bitter-sweet and haunting as this insubstantial pageant faded into reality.

There were other plays which Langham directed as skilfully: *The Taming of the*

*Shrew* in 1962, *Coriolanus* in 1961 and *Antony and Cleopatra* in 1967, all with the same meticulous attention to text and yet bright, innovative ideas of staging. Langham got his theatrical effects brilliantly, but he never sacrificed the dramatic values to do so.

All this time, the festival was expanding, music having been joined with drama right from the start. But whether it was *The Taming of the Shrew* or *King Lear*, *A Soldier's Tale* by Stravinsky or *The Mikado*, the visual and artistic standards were the same.

Indeed Canada had never seen such costumes or properties. In the history plays particularly, silks and satins and heraldic devices dazzled the eye; the baptism scene in *Henry VIII* brought gasps of delight from the audience. The caskets in *The Merchant of Venice*, the dinner-party ware in *Timon of Athens*, the ceremonial cross in *King John* and, above all, the masks in *Oedipus Rex*, were marvels of the designer's art and the property-makers' craft.

In this, Tyrone Guthrie's dream and Tanya Moiseiwitsch's reality combined to re-establish Shakespeare's own intent: that the opulence of costume, the staging of processions, the mock-play of battles would make audiences goggle and gasp with delight, projecting a larger-than-life visual image on the outside to convey the larger-than-life emotions on the inside. For the purpose of playing, as Shakespeare knew and Hamlet didn't, is not to hold a mirror up to nature, but to put it under a magnifying glass. The jealousy of an Othello, the eccentricity of a Lear, the gullibility of a Malvolio are beyond human scope and, as Coleridge says, make us exercise that "willing suspension of disbelief which constitutes poetic faith".

Because of such direction, such design and such playing, the audiences grew. Indeed, people could scarcely wait for the next season and it was advanced from July into June and lengthened from August into September.

No wonder. Where else in the world, let alone Canada, could people see, as they were able to in 1965, both parts of *Henry IV* and *Julius Caesar* by Shakespeare and *The Cherry Orchard* by Chekhov, all on the Festival stage; Mozart's *Marriage of Figaro* and Kurt Weill's *The Rise and Fall of the City Mahagonny* in a nearby proscenium theatre, the Avon, and hear, in concert on successive weekends, Claudio Arrau, Jean-Pierre Rampal, Elizabeth Benson Guy, Lois Marshall, the Festival Singers, the Mendelssohn Choir plus the Dave Brubeck Quartet and Benny Goodman?

Such organic growth, moreover, had always had the audience in mind. While attempting, and often achieving, the highest possible standards of production and performance, the Stratford Festival had kept its eye firmly on the box-office.

That is why, for example, the Festival put on *King John*, *A Midsummer Night's Dream* and *Romeo and Juliet* in 1960 – a little-known but gorgeously costumed history play, a popular comedy and a favourite tragedy. But at the same time the Avon, a proscenium stage made over from a movie house, was rented by the Festival to mount a Guthrie-directed *H.M.S. Pinafore* by Gilbert and Sullivan – a production which, for those used to amateur performances of G & S in high-school auditoriums, was as big a revelation as Shakespeare in modern dress or Sophocles in authentic masks and buskins. So successful was *H.M.S. Pinafore* that for the next four years the company ran through the Gilbert and Sullivan favourites: *The Pirates of Penzance*, *The Gondoliers*, *The Mikado* and *The Yeoman of the Guard*.

In 1963 the festival directors, realizing the value of a proscenium stage alternative, bought the Avon and refurbished it. It has been an integral part of the festival ever since, and has seen memorable productions of Chekhov, Beckett, Strindberg, Ibsen, Sheridan, Coward, Wilde and Offenbach.

In 1968 Jean Gascon, the creator of the first permanent theatre in French Canada, Le Théâtre du Nouveau Monde, was appointed artistic director to replace Michael Langham. Gascon was a flamboyant actor, trained in the French and English classical traditions. He had acted at Stratford in 1956 in Langham's bi-cultural *Henry V*; had brought the Nouveau Monde's production of Molière's *Le Malade Imaginaire* to the festival in 1958 and had directed a successful *Othello* there in 1959.

His particular flair in directing was very different from Langham's. Langham was a textual director, Gascon was a theatrical director. In 1964 he had, for example, directed *The Comedy of Errors* as a *commedia dell'arte* or Punchinello entertainment, with five Pantaloons acting as commentators and general theatrical factotums, putting the play within a play. For a comedy so absurd as *The Comedy of Errors* it was a legitimate directorial approach, although the device created as many problems as it solved. Such an attitude keeps audiences off-balance and intrigued, not a bad approach so long as the director does not come to think himself a better playwright than the man who originally wrote the play.

What Gascon did, in his seven-year tenure as artistic director, was to make the festival even more popular, in the best sense of the word. He did not choose well-known plays, but he mined little-known plays for their theatrical content and gave them popular appeal.

So Ben Jonson's *The Alchemist*, Webster's *The Duchess of Malfi* and de Musset's *Lorenzaccio* had romping productions under his hand, together with Jonson's *Volpone* (directed by David William) and, at the Avon Theatre, farces by Feydeau and Labiche and a sumptuous, totally uproarious staging of Offenbach's *La Vie Parisienne*. Gascon also brought Molière to Stratford, this time in English: *Le Bourgeois Gentilhomme* in 1964; *Tartuffe* in '68, revived in '69; and *The Imaginary Invalid* in 1974.

Colourful, energetic, full of bounce, Gascon's productions did not please the scholars always, but they mightily pleased the public. It was as well, though, that he had John Hirsch, the co-founder of the Manitoba Theatre Centre, as his co-artistic director during part of his tenure.

Hirsch was in the Langham tradition: a man who respected the text, directing as unobtrusively as possible, helping the author, trying to let the play make its own points. He had made his mark in 1965 with a seemingly impossible task: putting Chekhov's *The Cherry Orchard* on the thrust-stage of the Festival Theatre. No one who saw that will ever forget the sounds of the axe offstage as the lights slowly dimmed: it was a requiem for Imperial Russia as moving as any lowering curtain might have made it.

The next year he tackled *Henry VI*. It proved, unfortunately, caviar to the general; it was a critical success but a great loss at the box-office. After that *Richard III* in 1967 was a plum both for him as director, with Alan Bates as Richard, and for audiences. He imposed a well thought out, meaningful interpretation of the play which reduced some of Shakespeare's youthful eccentricities in the writing.

Under Gascon and Hirsch the festival grew from 18 weeks with 217 performances in 1968 to 23 weeks with 357 performances in 1974. It toured major cities in the United

States as well as in Canada; it did a seven-month season for the National Arts Centre's opening year in 1969-70; it played in Copenhagen, Utrecht, The Hague, Warsaw, Krakow, Moscow and Leningrad in 1973, to huge excitement and acclaim, and went "down under" in 1974 for performances in Perth, Melbourne, Adelaide and Sydney.

During this time a new artistic director, Robin Phillips, was learning the company's ways, investigating the lively theatre across the country which in many ways had sprung from Stratford's success and pondering just what he would do when he replaced Gascon in June 1975.

Phillips was, and is, a phenomenon. Trained at England's Bristol Old Vic as actor and designer, as well as director, he had several objectives in mind when he took over the festival. The first, he said in 1974, was

> ...the linking of the Festival's stages in terms of overall philosophy so as to dispel any idea of a hierarchy of stages, with one enjoying status above or below the other....that each of the three stages have a separate and recognizable identity emerging naturally from within the company rather than inspired from without.

Three stages because, in 1971, a former curling rink (latterly a badminton court) belonging to the municipality was rented for the presentation of experimental work, workshop productions and chamber opera. This stage was necessary also to give an outlet for Canadian works, thus pacifying those writers who were bitter about the amount of money spent on Shakespeare and the classics at the country's leading theatre. It also appeased the granting agencies, who were on the receiving end of criticism from the same frustrated writers.

The second was to alter the original shape of the festival stage. Said Phillips:

> The idea was revolutionary. The stage itself was revolutionary. And the theatre experience came as a revelation. The Stratford experience forced everyone involved in theatre around the world to rethink and revise ideas that had been nurtured on the proscenium arch. Today, the wheel has come full circle, and the challenge lies in rethinking and revising ideas nurtured on the experience of the past twenty-one years.

Tanya Moiseiwitsch was thus commissioned to make the balcony movable, leaving the whole stage free for productions. For though a balcony is necessary in some plays (*Antony and Cleopatra*, *Romeo and Juliet*, *Troilus and Cressida* and *The Tempest*, for example), it is a nuisance in others.

The third was to form a company of actors, on a three-year contract, which would be able to put on Shakespearean productions at the Avon and on the Third Stage and also tour them, thus making Stratford a truly national theatre. To direct these players, Phillips also planned to hire directors from regional theatres across the country. These would not only be challenged by the Stratford style in the summer, but might give the touring company a welcome in winter when they arrived in the regional theatres, preferably within the subscription series.

Concerned as he was with making Stratford a national theatre in fact as well as name, in visibility as well as quality, Phillips was not as chauvinistic as some of the detractors who had pursued him virulently in the press during his first, pre-season year. He would, and did, make stars out of Canadian actors, but he would, and did, bring stars in from other countries. His first major coup in his tenure was to bring Maggie Smith to Stratford. A highly respected stage actress, and an Oscar-winner in films, Maggie Smith was delighted to come to work in a true theatrical company. So was Brian Bedford, another British actor who had also worked in the U.S. where he had won a Tony and the Los Angeles Drama Critics' Award. Jessica Tandy and Hume Cronyn came in from New York, but the Cronyn family is native to London, Ontario, just thirty miles down the road from Stratford; for them it was a pleasant return, as it had been in 1969 when Hume Cronyn played the title role in Peter Luke's *Hadrian VII*.

Having laid out the guidelines, Phillips proceeded to implement them. A separate company of actors was put together for a pre-festival tour of the two early comedies, *The Comedy of Errors* and *The Two Gentlemen of Verona*, both directed by Phillips. One was set in the American West, one in what seemed to be a pretty decadent part of the Italian Riviera; the costumes were simple, and vague in their period. All of this left the actors to make their own way. Their tour was successful, their festival season a triumph. Both shows closed at 82% of capacity at the Avon.

There was a new style in the acting, a physical energy the more noticeable because of the simple sets and costumes. (Turning a somersault in tights is easier than in a swathing robe of hempen homespun.) There was also a textually careful but not entirely traditional attitude to the plays at the Festival Theatre stage. *Measure for Measure* was done in twentieth-century formal dress, and Martha Henry, Brian Bedford, William Hutt and Richard Monette made modern sense out of that protean, somewhat muddled piece. *Twelfth Night*, only a century out of its time, the actors dressed in seventeenth-century lace collars and booted breeches, was immensely popular, with Brian Bedford giving a virtuoso performance of that sad character Malvolio, and Tom Kneebone making a haunting figure of the Fool.

There was now a spaciousness on the stage, the balcony being removed, that was matched by a breadth of vision, an attention to detail and a mastery of the textual material which gave Phillips in his first season an extra 30,000 in the audience and almost a quarter of a million dollars more at the box-office. More, it gave a new excitement and spirit to the festival which was to build throughout his career.

He directed Maggie Smith as Lady Macbeth in a production of that old war-horse which was effective purely because of the intensity of the playing and the violence of the stage business. He directed her in *As You Like It*, where she became a captivating boy roaming the Forest of Arden in clothes not seen until a hundred years after Shakespeare's death, and in *Much Ado About Nothing*, where her Beatrice was a rapier-like foil to Brian Bedford's Benedick.

But the two parts everyone waited to see her play were Amanda Prynne in Noel Coward's *Private Lives* in 1978 (the same year as Lady Macbeth) and Virginia in Edna O'Brien's *Virginia*, based on the letters and diaries of Virginia Woolf, in 1980 (the same year as Beatrice).

As Amanda, Maggie Smith glittered as the consummate comedienne that she is, her voice inflected with all the proper mannerisms of the bright young things. But her true virtuosity was allowed to shine in *Virginia* with the minimum of fuss by the director. Her mercurial changes of tempo put the candour and the shabby gentility of Bloomsbury into its proper intellectual context, but her building from neurosis to suicidal depression was a presentation of universality which even Virginia Woolf's own craft lacked.

To bring the moderns – Coward, O'Brien and Wilde – into direct contest with Shakespeare on the thrust stage was typical of Phillips. But then Phillips took a gamble on everything but talent and intensity. He put *The Tempest* and *Hamlet* on at the Avon, and transferred a lavish musical based on Voltaire's *Candide* to the Festival Theatre. He alternated three people in the title role of *Richard II* one year and two in *Henry V* in another. He hired a dramaturge and produced a dozen or so original plays at the Third Stage, including two operas. He cast William Hutt as Lady Bracknell in *The Importance of Being Earnest* and Hutt at no time *seemed* like a man playing a woman (very Shakespearean, that). He not only produced *Titus Andronicus*, a blood-bedaubed tragedy not often presented even by Shakespearean theatres, but assigned Brian Bedford, a superb actor, to be its neophyte and highly successful director. He brought in directors from modern stages to try their hands at the Festival Stage. And in four seasons Phillips directed sixteen productions himself and was co-director for another eight.

In 1978, in the first week of the festival, there was a "gala evening" on Monday, and then on successive days, in the afternoon and evening, there were the première performances of *Macbeth*, *The Winter's Tale* and *As You Like It* in the Festival Theatre; John Whiting's *The Devils*, Chekhov's *Uncle Vanya* and the North American première of Barry Collins' *Judgement* at the Avon. By August these plays had been joined by *Titus Andronicus* and *Julius Caesar* at the Festival Theatre, *Heloise and Abelard*, *Private Lives* and *Candide* at the Avon, and seven more at the Third Stage. In 1979 there was equal richness and variety, and in 1980, his final year as artistic director, Phillips produced a programme with a collection of star actors which boggled the mind. Perhaps his most remarkable achievement was to persuade Peter Ustinov to play King Lear. An eccentric but believable and strong production, it sold out every seat in the 1979 season and again when it was revived in 1980.

By this time, too, a theatre school was being actively planned and an organization was being set up to produce films at Stratford using both the vibrant energies of the permanent company and the towering skill of Phillips as a director.

Yet, for all its bigness, its bustle and its international reputation, the Festival has not changed the town significantly. Writing in *The Stratford Scene 1958-68*, Berners Jackson – professor of English at McMaster University, organizer of the Stratford seminars and long time Festival board member – said:

> Stratford is as fortunate in what it has avoided as in what it has achieved. The parasitic growth of tourist trinketry, side shows and other enticements, that disfigures many a summer rendezvous has been frustrated by a policy that refuses to permit an irresponsible exploitation of the Festival. Just as one cannot gorge oneself on Hamletburgers or Shakespeare-shakes...so too there is nothing of the mock-Tudor about the place. The old town has kept the Shakespearean names for some of its wards and streets and schools that it bestowed on them long before the new theatre came there; these are part of the dignity it has retained while its development around the festival has been as unruffled and as comely as its river. New industry surrounds it, new prosperity invigorates it, but its essential character, to the visitor at least, appears unaltered.

So it does twelve years later.

Sitting on the island in the middle of the Avon this summer – officially named Tom Patterson Island a couple of years ago, with a modest bronze plaque to say so – I watched people walking in to a matinée. I let my mind's eye roam back over the twenty-eight years I have been coming to Stratford.

To the afternoon in the tent during 1954's *Measure for Measure* when someone in the back row shouted "Speak up, Mason" to James Mason playing Angelo. To the sizzling portrayal of Richard III by Brian Bedford in 1977. To the moment, in an early production of *Twelfth Night*, when Christopher Plummer as Andrew Aguecheek dropped vertically out of sight down the trapdoor in a piece of business which so convulsed the audience that it stopped the play for a solid minute. To those haunting axe-sounds chopping down *The Cherry Orchard*. To Martha Henry, in a rending emotional act, removing her veil at the end of 1976's *Measure for Measure*. To the astonishing beauty of Ginette Letondal as Katherine in the 1956 *Henry V*. To the two entire performances of *Cyrano de Bergerac*, with Christopher Plummer in the title role in 1962, and John Colicos in 1963. To the savagery of putting out Gloucester's eyes in Ustinov's *King Lear* in 1979.

But also to leisurely picnic dinners on that very island before an evening performance; to borrowing cuff-links one opening night from no less a person than Tom Patterson himself; to listening one magical Sunday night in 1973 to the New York Brass playing under the trees near the theatre after a whole day's musical programme entitled simply "Music for a Summer Day" – a day which had included an afternoon concert by the Chicago Symphony, and an evening recital by Philippe Entremont.

Above all, to driving home year after year in the moonlight, through standing silvered corn, wondering, by my troth, what we all did till the Stratford Festival came along.

# The Stratford Festival

1    *Barbara Bryne as a fearsome*
*Duchess of York in* **Richard III**, *1967*

1    *The sweet nurse played by Kate Reid in* **Romeo and Juliet**, *1960*

2    *Louise Marleau and Christopher Walken as the young lovers in a later (1968) production of* **Romeo and Juliet**

3   *Lewis Gordon as a rollicking*
*Falstaff in* **Henry IV: Part Two**

1  *William Hutt as Falstaff dis-
comfited in* The Merry Wives of
Windsor

2  *Tony van Bridge as Falstaff is
cajoled into quietness by Anna
Wing as Mistress Quickly in the 1967*
Merry Wives of Windsor

**3**  *Two merry wives, played by Frances Hyland as Mistress Ford and Zoë Caldwell as Mistress Page in the 1967 production*

**4**  **As You Like It**, *1978, with Jack Wetherall as Orlando, Peter Hutt as Silvius, Patricia Idlette as Phebe and Maggie Smith as Rosalind*

**5**  *From an earlier (1972)* **As You Like It**, *Pamela Brook as Celia, Edward Atienza as Touchstone and Carole Shelley as Rosalind*

1    *Alec Guinness as the King of France, Irene Worth as Helena in the 1953 production of* **All's Well That Ends Well** *that opened the Stratford Festival*

2    **Timon of Athens**, *1963. Tony van Bridge as Sempronius, Leo Ciceri as Lucullus, Mervyn Blake as Lucius, William Hutt as Alcibiades*

3    *The set and costumes designed by Daphne Dare for* **Measure for Measure** *in 1975*

4

5

6

4    *William Needles as Petruchio makes an unorthodox arrival in a Wild West version of* **The Taming of the Shrew**, *1954*

5    *Richard McMillan as Sir Andrew Aguecheek shows his appreciation for Kate Reid as Maria; Barry MacGregor as Sir Toby Belch in* **Twelfth Night**, *1980*

6    *The letter scene from* **Love's Labour's Lost**, *1961. Murray Scott as Moth, Paul Scofield as Don Adriano*

1    *Maggie Smith as Beatrice,
Brian Bedford as Benedick in* **Much
Ado About Nothing**, *1980*

2    *Titania played by Maggie Smith
caresses Bottom played by Alan
Scarfe in* **A Midsummer Night's
Dream**, *1977*

3    *From the same 1977 produc-
tion, Maggie Smith as Hippolyta,
Martha Henry as Helena, Domini
Blythe as Hermia*

4    *William Hutt as Prospero casts
his eerie spells over the dark island
set designed for* **The Tempest** *at the
Avon Theatre, 1976*

1    *Hume Cronyn as Shylock, the much-maligned Jewish money-lender in* The Merchant of Venice, *1976*

2    *Desmond Heeley's costume design for Gremio in the 1973 pro-duction of* The Taming of the Shrew

3    *Another Shylock played by Frederick Valk in 1955*

**4**   *Paul Scofield in the title role,*
Coriolanus, *1961*

1    *Peter Ustinov as a grieving
Lear, Ingrid Blekys as Cordelia in*
**King Lear**, *1979*

2    *Peter Ustinov repeating his role
of Lear in 1980 with William Hutt as
the Fool*

3    *William Hutt as Lear in this
1972 production howls at the storm
as Edward Atienza's Fool crouches
in terror at his feet*

1    *From a 1972 production of*
**King Lear**. *William Hutt as King
Lear, Powys Thomas as Gloucester*

**2**

2    *Pat Galloway, Rita Howell and
Amelia Hall as the three Witches of
the 1962* **Macbeth**

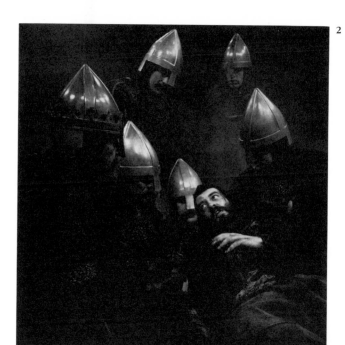

1   *Douglas Rain in the title role,*
*Maggie Smith as Lady Macbeth in*
**Macbeth***, 1978*

2   *From the same production of*
**Macbeth***, Rod Beattie as a wounded*
*captain with members of the cast*

3   *Christopher Plummer, Eleanor*
*Stuart and Ginette Letondal in the*
*betrothal scene from* **Henry V***, 1956*

1   *Richard Monette as* **Henry V**
*with members of the company, 1980,*
*alternating the role during the sea-*
*son with Jack Wetherall*

2   *Jack Wetherall in the same*
*scene from the 1980 production of*
**Henry V**

**3**  *Richard Monette as Hamlet,*
*Richard Partington as Laertes duel*
*before the court in* **Hamlet***, 1976*

1    *Alan Bates as Richard, Duke of Gloucester in the 1967 production of* **Richard III**

2    *Stephen Russell in the title role of* **Richard II**, *1979*

3    *Alec Guinness evil-featured and hunchbacked as King Richard III in the original (1953) Stratford Festival production*

**4**   *The coronation scene with Alec Guinness and members of the cast*

**5**   *A later (1977) production of* **Richard III**. *In the foreground, Maggie Smith as Queen Elizabeth, Margaret Tyzack as Queen Margaret and Brian Bedford as Richard*

1    *The baptism of Elizabeth the First in* **Henry VIII**. *Douglas Rain as Cardinal Wolsey and Douglas Campbell as the King*

2    *Margot Dionne as Lady Percy, Stephen Russell as Harry Percy (Hotspur) in* **Henry IV: Part One**, *1979*

**3**  *Helen Carey as Lady Teazle, Robin Gammell as Joseph Surface in Richard Sheridan's* **School for Scandal**, *1970*

**4**  *The three Surfaces, Barry MacGregor as Charles, Mervyn Blake as Sir Oliver, Robin Gammell as Joseph in the same production*

**5**  *Dawn Greenhalgh as Beline, William Hutt as Argan in Molière's* **The Imaginary Invalid**, *1974*

**1** **Tartuffe**, *Molière's play on religious hypocrisy, with William Hutt in the title role, 1969*

**2** *Oscar Wilde's* **The Importance Of Being Earnest**, *1976. William Hutt as the imperious and totally believable Lady Bracknell*

**3** *Kate Reid as the indomitable Henny in* **Bosoms and Neglect** *by John Guare, 1980*

4    *Patricia Conolly as Vita, Maggie Smith as Virginia in Edna
O'Brien's* **Virginia**, *1980*

5    *Daphne Dare's design for Mrs
Millamant's costume in* **The Way of
the World** *by William Congreve,
1976*

6    *The actual costume worn by
Maggie Smith*

1    *Cyrano and his famous nose,
Christopher Plummer in the 1962
production of* **Cyrano de Bergerac**
*by Edmond Rostand*

2    *Kate Reid as Fonsia, Douglas
Rain as Weller in* **The Gin Game** *by
D. L. Coburn, 1980*

3

4

3    *A lesson in the pronunciation of vowels. Douglas Rain as Jourdain, Mervyn Blake as the Philosopher in Molière's* **Le Bourgeois Gentilhomme**, *1964*

4    *Bertolt Brecht's* **Trumpets and Drums**, *1975. William Hutt as Captain Brazen, Gordon Pinsent as Captain Plume in the urinal scene*

1    *Jennifer Phipps as Mrs Peachum, Graeme Campbell as Mr Peachum and Edda Gaborek as their daughter Polly in John Gay's* **The Beggar's Opera**, *1980*

2    *Barry MacGregor as Dobchinsky in* **The Government Inspector** *by Nikolai Gogol, 1967*

3    *Tony van Bridge as the Mayor in the same production of Gogol's satire of corrupt officialdom*

4    *The boisterous ladies of the town in a lively scene from* **The Beggar's Opera**, *1980*

5    *In contrasting style the Royal Winnipeg Ballet performing* **Rose Latulippe** *choreographed by Brian Macdonald, 1966*

1    *William Hutt as Vanya in
Anton Chekhov's* **Uncle Vanya**, *1978*

2    *William Hutt as the avaricious
Volpone in Ben Jonson's* **Volpone**, *a
1971 production*

3 *Reluctant duellists Rod Beattie as Silvio and Goldie Semple as Beatrice in* **The Servant of Two Masters** *by Carlo Goldoni, 1980*

**1** *Douglas Rain as John Aubrey in Patrick Garland's* **Brief Lives**, *adapted from the writings of John Aubrey*

**2** *Martha Henry as Sister Jeanne in John Whiting's* **The Devils** *based on a book by Aldous Huxley, 1978*

**3** *The torture of Father Grandier played by Nicholas Pennell in* **The Devils** *by John Whiting*

1 *Powys Thomas as Vladimir,
Eric Donkin as Estragon, Adrian
Pecknold as Lucky, James Blendick
as Pozzo in Samuel Beckett's* Wait-
ing for Godot, *1968*

**2** *Gilbert and Sullivan's* **H. M. S. Pinafore,** *a 1960 production*

**3** *Another Gilbert and Sullivan favourite,* **The Mikado,** *1963*

1  *Tony van Bridge as Falstaff tor-*
*mented by the fiends of Herne Hill*
*in* **The Merry Wives of Windsor**,
*1967*

2    *The great masked figures
designed by Tanya Moiseiwitsch for
Sophocles'* **Oedipus Rex**, *1954.
James Mason played the King*

1    *The remarkable Skip Manley (centre) in overalls and straw hat supervising the raising of the tent*

2    *Many local inhabitants considered the raising and lowering of the tent to be Stratford's best entertainment*

THE STRATFORD FESTIVAL   85

1    *Aerial view of the Festival Theatre under construction, 1953, the bowl-like amphitheatre reminiscent of an ancient Greek theatre*

2    *The huge canvas tent that covered a concrete auditorium and stage for an amazing four seasons*

3     *The Festival Theatre stage after 1975, slightly changed since the original design by Tyrone Guthrie and Tanya Moiseiwitsch*

1     *The High Victorian style does not seem to jar with the new Tudor interest in Stratford. The Perth County Courthouse with its adjacent Italianate dovecot has its own serenity*

2     *The Meighen Memorial Garden gives an English flavour to the Festival Theatre in Ontario's Stratford*

**3**   *The Stratford Festival glows
across the artificial lake – with
Shakespeare inside, late summer
outside*

# The Shaw Festival

NIAGARA-ON-THE-LAKE *is a patrician place. Let the honeymooners and gawkers go to Niagara Falls, a dozen miles away; the rich would always come to Niagara-on-the-Lake. John Graves Simcoe, the first governor of Upper Canada, made it his capital in 1792. When the skirmishes between new Americans and old imperialists were over, Americans came across the border to build large, beautifully designed summer homes there. For over a century they and their Canadian fellows have protected it and made it a sanctuary of dignified living.*

*St. Mark's Church goes back to Queen Anne in spirit and design; many of the other public buildings are High Victorian. But the buildings are secondary to the gardens and the trees, huge trees, which give welcome shade in which to enjoy the breezes coming in cool from Lake Ontario.*

*On either side of the town, parkland, designed and laid out* during the 1930's, gives the public the same facilities as the private persons have in their shadowed houses. The orderliness of it, the greenness, make it a picnic spot of immense charm and unobtrusive facility.

But there surely should be more for the people in such a place than walking the main street and buying in the boutiques. So thought Brian Doherty, a local lawyer who was dotty about theatre and who, as a result, dreamed up the Shaw Festival. The origins of the idea are detailed in his book typically entitled *Not Bloody Likely*. On a cold February evening (it is not *always* summer, even in Niagara-on-the-Lake) a friend had invited a group in after dinner for coffee and brandy.

> Gathered round the fire we chatted. Soon all of us were absorbed in our favourite topic: the beauty and charm of Niagara-on-the-Lake and the fact that its historic heritage was being threatened.
>
> "Let's do something," I said at one point in the long evening of talk. "Instead of worrying and criticizing let's do something for the town we love, something we believe in."
>
> "How about theatre?" It was a New York actress who made that suggestion.
>
> "Shaw!" I suddenly exclaimed. After all these years of gestation, the idea seemed to explode in my head. "Shaw. Shaw would be wonderful."
>
> I started to build on the notion: "We'd have to make it really professional, something like Shakespeare in Stratford. We couldn't be just another stock company. It would have to be more than that."
>
> "But where in the world would we stage it?" someone sensibly asked.
>
> The historic nineteenth-century Court House came immediately to mind.

Only a visionary like Doherty, a flamboyant, theatre-obsessed man, could really have believed that the Court House could become a theatre. It had a flat floor, no seats, no stage and little ventilation. It did have an imposing façade; it was in the main street opposite the landmark clock-tower; it was, he found out, available.

And so, on Friday June 29, 1962, the Shaw Festival was born, with a performance of the Hell Scene from *Man and Superman* – on a sweltering humid night which made the Court House an appropriate though uncomfortable location for it.

The seats in that theatre were hard, the sight-lines terrible. But the choice of plays, the calibre of the actors and the ingenuity of Andrew Allan, the first artistic director, drew more and more people to it.

In 1963, after an initial performance of *Spring Thaw* to raise money, the season offered *How He Lied to her Husband*, *The Man of Destiny* and *Androcles and the Lion*. In 1964, *Heartbreak House*, *Village Wooing*, *The Dark Lady of the Sonnets* and *John Bull's Other Island*. In 1965, *Pygmalion* and *The Millionairess* plus Sean O'Casey's *The Shadow of a Gunman* – the latter the first play by a Shaw contemporary, and a natural for a festival director named Doherty and an assistant artistic director called Sean Mulcahy.

With growing audiences, improvements to the theatre (air conditioning in 1963, raised seating in 1964) and a genuine interest from the critics of the metropolitan papers in Toronto and elsewhere, the festival was jogging along well.

Then came the thunderbolt. For the fifth season, Doherty hired Barry Morse as artistic director. Again, let him tell his story.

Working with Barry was like going over Niagara Falls in a barrel. In the early part of the season, when Barry was still filming his television series *The Fugitive* he was a man in constant motion. I remember one occasion when Ray Wickens and I drove him from Niagara-on-the-Lake to Toronto to catch a plane. During the drive he overwhelmed us with a long list of suggestions about publicity, ticket sales, staff, remodelling and redecorating the theatre – a hundred details about a dozen matters. He was still shouting last-minute brain waves as he rushed to board the plane. We drove back to Niagara-on-the-Lake bemused. I'd hardly had a chance to settle down at home when the telephone rang. It was Barry. He had just landed in California and must communicate to me at once a new flood of ideas and suggestions.

For his season – the season which put the Shaw Festival firmly on the map – Morse chose three plays: *Man and Superman*, *Misalliance* and *The Apple Cart*.

His casting was superb and the troupe of actors he assembled was a *Who's Who* of the Canadian theatre: Betty Leighton, Pat Galloway, Tom Kneebone, Patrick Boxill, Leslie Yeo, Hugh Webster; and two who were not Canadian, but who were to make enormous reputations in Canada: Paxton Whitehead and Zoë Caldwell.

The performances by these latter in *The Apple Cart* upset the town's apple cart. For it, and the other plays, led to a virtually sold-out season, to notices in newspapers in Montreal, Winnipeg and Calgary as well as in many papers in the United States. People flocked to see the plays, some bringing their picnics with them, but many crowding into the Oban Inn and the Prince of Wales Hotel for dinner and jamming the streets before and after.

Such support led the Festival to think seriously of building a real theatre, and led the retired residents to wonder if they wanted one. Tourists who came and went were one thing; tourists who stayed several days, or came in busloads to fill the dining-rooms of the town's two favourite hotels, were something else.

But the momentum of the festival itself was not to be stopped. Paxton Whitehead was already a consummate actor when he came to Niagara-on-the-Lake; he stayed to become a shrewd, volatile artistic director who, following in Morse's giant footsteps, turned this small, quaint additional tourist attraction into a major festival which no one who loved theatre in Ontario's golden triangle would dare miss.

In his first four years he brought such Shavian masterpieces as *Arms and the Man*, *You Never Can Tell*, *Major Barbara*, *The Doctor's Dilemma* and *The Philanderer* to the Court House with casts including Diana Barrington, Louise Marleau, James Valentine, Jennifer Phipps, Alan Scarfe, Frances Hyland, Martha Henry, Heath Lamberts, Tony van Bridge and – inspired choice – Stanley Holloway, octogenarian veteran of British vaude- ville and pantomime. Holloway played Candida's father Burgess and, as one critic said, gambolled "through his part with an astonishing verve and sprightliness" – meaning that he made most of his lines up as he went along. The critic of New York's *Village Voice* said of Heath Lamberts' performance in *Misalliance*:

Mr. Lamberts is hard to describe: imagine a bowl of Jello putting on airs, yet about to burst into tears at any moment. He is one rotund tremor of fear and puppy fat, playing scales of hysteria at varied volumes on his voice, and playing every comic stunt stage tradition has sanctified for nervous gunsels, cocking his revolver only to have the front half fall down etc.... This performance is a real stage creation; he manages to travel the main lines of Shaw's speeches, but gives you a recognizable and comic human being in between them.

Such playing by such actors had the tiny Court House sold out night after night despite its lack of sophisticated stage machinery for the actors, and its buttock-numbing seats for the audience. People were being turned away. A new theatre, therefore, was essential.

One site with excellent access, a view over the lake and plenty of space was found, but the town council would not release the land. Two other sites were surveyed, both belonging to the federal government; one was not available, the other was vigorously opposed by members of the adjacent golf club, one of whom chased Doherty off the place with a putter. City land next to the Court House was next considered, plans drawn and an architect's conceptual design actually made. But zoning changes, rights-of-way, municipal services and such were all fought tooth-and-nail by those residents who opposed the festival.

By December 1971 a perfect site, two blocks from the Court House, near the hospital and not too close to any houses, had been chosen. The rights had to be negotiated from such diverse bodies as the local hospital, the golf club, the town council, the Boy Scouts and even the federal department of Indian Affairs and Native Development (whose present title belies its ancient ties with a southern, non-Indian settlement). Eighteen months later, on a glowering June day which finally lapsed into an inconveniently steamy drizzle, the new theatre was opened. Designed by Ron Thom – an architect who had made his name with two dazzling academic projects, Massey College in Toronto and Trent University in Peterborough – the theatre, all cosy red brick and natural cedar, sat comfortably in its newly landscaped setting, among some of Niagara-on-the-Lake's magnificent trees.

But it takes more than a sylvan setting to hide the essential ugliness of any theatre which is basically two boxes, one longways for the audience, the other vertical for the stage crew and actors. Thom solved the problem by flinging out galleries round the base of the audience's box, all glass and cedar strakes, and then, within the same plane and using the same angles of roof and siding, stepping the high stage box down with a scenery workshop, wardrobe, workshop and mechanical housing, all on different levels.

The resulting theatre is a neat graft into the loveliness of the place, at once imposing and welcoming – a sort of natural full stop to the Niagara Parks Commission's scenic drive on one side, and the town's distinguished Main Street on the other.

Theatre-goers were impressed when they got inside, on that first night. Blessedly soft seats with enough leg-room for all but the tallest, ranged in rows with impeccable sight-lines in a pale cedar interior; rough cedar which, though a threat to the passing silks and baratheas of the elegant first-nighters, was a sponge to soak up sound. Paxton Whitehead had long insisted that Shaw's witty words be thrown clearly and resoundingly into the listener's ears and mind – now the acoustics made it possible.

Said Clive Barnes in the *New York Times*:

Now in its 12th season, the Shaw Festival last week played its trump card. It is a new 830-seat theatre, and it is one of the loveliest in North America.

Stanley Holloway remarked before the curtain went up on *You Never Can Tell*: "There are no laughs or applause soaked into the walls yet; we've got to put those in." He,

Paxton Whitehead, Mary Savidge, James Valentine and Domini Blythe did exactly that, on that and succeeding nights – with *You Never Can Tell*, *Fanny's First Play* and *The Brass Butterfly* by William (*Lord of the Flies*) Golding.

Entertainment: that's what the Shaw Festival has always tried to provide, and under its present artistic director, Christopher Newton, that's what it is still committed to providing. Not froth. Not straw-hat mindless farce. But witty, uncompromisingly well-done comedy, by either Shaw or his contemporaries.

Take the 1979 season as an example. *You Never Can Tell* was back again for its third production. Its ingredients are a mild satire on women's lib, the liberated woman being a successful writer of do-it-yourself psychology; a somewhat harsh condemnation of the Victorian *paterfamilias*, whose position as head of the house leads him into tyranny and, naturally, to separation from the liberated woman; a playful look at the genteel poverty of the beginning professional (in this play, a dentist) and a hilarious analysis of the Edwardian class system, fleshed out in a father who is a waiter and a son who is a successful barrister. Played by such actors as Leslie Yeo (acting artistic director for the season), Gillie Fenwick and Mary Savidge, with Christopher Gaze and Mary Haney as two believable but impossible children, the show rocked the house night after night.

*Captain Brassbound's Conversion* is Shaw in his sillier, less attractive mode. The medium is used merely for Shaw's usual anti-establishment message, and the play palls. A scene in the Moorish castle was unashamedly camped up and the third act was mere Gilbert and Sullivan without music.

*Village Wooing*, an hour-long *jeu d'esprit* much beloved by Shavian addicts, was staged beautifully at the Court House Theatre, which is still doing yeoman service for shorter pieces where the strain on the spectator's neck – and seat – is obviously less.

Two plays about Shaw – *My Astonishing Self* and *Dear Liar* – also ran in the Court House, both to excellent critical notices and impressive box-office. And for those who did not want solely Shaw, there was Emlyn Williams' *The Corn is Green* and Noel Coward's *Blithe Spirit*.

Entertainment. Whenever the Shaw Festival forgets that, forgets the holiday spirit of its surrounding parks, forgets that 40% of its box-office comes from American tourists – and the rest from Canadian ones – it falters. It faltered in 1978 with Ibsen. The play was *John Gabriel Borkman*, a grim play about a thwarted capitalist. Borkman's grandiose scheme for putting together money to grubstake those who would find uranium and nickel and oil collapses; he is declared bankrupt and he is convicted, unfairly but legally, as an embezzler. Douglas Campbell, a superb actor, gave a superb performance. So did Frances Hyland and other good actors in less important roles. But the play did not fit the mood of the festival, however well the cast played their roles. When the Ibsen piece closed part way through the season, only half the available seats had been sold.

On the other hand, *Thark*, a farce by Ben Travers which ran for years in England's West End, was almost a sell-out the year before. And so was J. M. Barrie's *The Admirable Crichton* in an earlier year.

The high point of the festival so far, for me anyway – and I've seen a good many of its productions – has been *Man and Superman*, Shaw's five-hour-long play about the Life Force, which was presented in 1977. The Life Force is concerned with Shaw's quaint Fabian notion, going back to John Stuart Mill and other Victorian thinkers, that man is slowly but surely advancing to perfection. After two world wars, the holocaust in Nazi Germany, and Vietnam, a modern audience cannot believe that. But Shaw, at the turn of the century, did.

Not that perfectibility is Shaw's only outdated idea; in *Man and Superman*, Shaw maintains that the procreation of children, especially by those who are themselves of good blood-lines, will somehow lead to a world of superbeings. (Procreation is not an idea to grab a modern audience either.) When, for example, Violet Robinson, the young, liberated female in the play, is thought to be pregnant while still unmarried, all the conventional people take the conventional attitude and her brother, a romantic who idealizes women, bursts into tears. But John Tanner, proponent of the Life Force, rebukes him:

> Good Heavens, man, what are you crying for? Here is a woman whom we all supposed to be making bad water-colour sketches, practising Grieg and Brahms, gadding about to concerts and parties, wasting her life and her money. We suddenly learn that she has turned from these sillinesses to the fulfilment of her highest purpose and greatest function – to increase, multiply, and replenish the earth. And instead of admiring her courage and rejoicing in her instinct; instead of crowning the completed womanhood and raising the triumphal strain of "Unto us a child is born: unto us a son is given," here you are – you who have been as merry as grigs in your mourning for the dead – all pulling long faces and looking as ashamed and disgraced as if the girl had committed the vilest of crimes.

That kind of outrageous, witty incisive preaching is Shaw. And in the Hell Scene of *Man and Superman* he puts forth more and more of his ideas, until the complete play stretches for five hours. The part of John Tanner is about double in length that of King Lear or Hamlet, but Ian Richardson, an actor imported from the Royal Shakespeare Company in England, played it without faltering.

Fourteen of the twenty-five performances at Niagara-on-the-Lake were of the whole five-hour show as Shaw wrote it. Between Acts II and III there was an extended intermission, during which the audience were served refreshments (by the women's auxiliary of the Festival) as they sat out on the lawns and terraces.

As we sat there on one of those remarkable afternoons my companion said to me: "Just think, twenty-five years ago the only theatre in this country at this time of the year was a straw-hat circuit playing Broadway and West End comedies old enough to be available at reasonable royalty. Now we are sitting here in a superb setting and going back, after I've finished my gin and tonic, into an equally superb theatre to watch one of the very great plays in the English language done by a cast of real excellence. I can scarcely wait to go back and get on with it. It almost makes you believe that the Life Force is taking us onwards and upwards after all."

It does indeed. Every season I feel that about the Shaw Festival. Doherty's vision has become reality. The parks are still there; the town has not, despite the doomsayers, become overcrowded, and the presence of the theatre is not obtrusive, though its reputation is now international. Not that you will think of that when you drive out there, late on a summer afternoon, to have a picnic and go to the current play. To the chilled wine, the cold chicken and salad you have brought with you, add fresh cherries or strawberries or raspberries from the fruit stands that dot the approaches (in very controlled, Parks Commission settings, of course). Then spread your own table (municipally provided) before you go to listen to some of the most elegant, apparently logical nonsense ever written in English.

Or, if it pleases you better, book a table at the Oban Inn, and dine on the verandah overlooking the glinting lake and the lush golf course. There you may have a cold soup called Curry Sheba – which everyone should taste at least once in life – poached fresh salmon and home-made mayonnaise, dessert and coffee, all served with no appearance of haste and bustle yet guaranteed to get you out in time for the curtain.

Mrs. Simcoe, whose husband chose Niagara-on-the-Lake as his capital, might not approve of Shaw's views; but with all the social events and picnicking and jollity that surround it, she would certainly approve of the Shaw Festival.

# The Shaw Festival

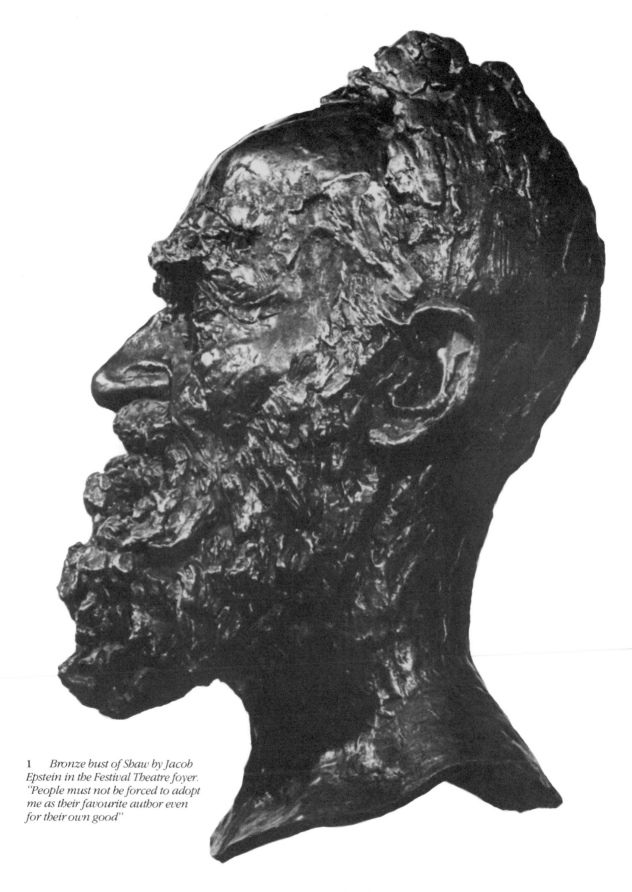

1   *Bronze bust of Shaw by Jacob
Epstein in the Festival Theatre foyer.
"People must not be forced to adopt
me as their favourite author even
for their own good"*

**1**   *Donal Donnelly as a convincing George Bernard Shaw in Michael Voysey's* **My Astonishing Self**, *1979*

**2** *Paxton Whitehead in the title role of Brandon Thomas'* **Charley's Aunt**, *1974*

**3** *Paxton Whitehead as Lord Fancourt Babberley, John Horton as Charley Wykeham, James Valentine as Jack Chesney in the same production*

1    *Shaw's* **Getting Married**, *1972.*
*Heath Lamberts as Sinjon Hotchkiss,*
*Noel Howlett as the Bishop, Moya*
*Fenwick as Mrs George*

2    *From the same production of*
**Getting Married**, *Noel Howlett as*
*the Bishop, Betty Leighton as Mrs*
*Bridgenorth, 'Wenna Shaw as Leo,*
*Ronald Drake as General Bridgenorth,*
*Heath Lamberts as Sinjon Hotchkiss*
*and (standing) Michael Hogan as*
*Cecil Sykes*

3    *Merrilyn Gann as "Z" and Jack*
*Medley as "A" in Shaw's* **Village**
**Wooing**, *1979*

4 *Carole Shelley as Cherry Buck, Lynne Griffin as Kitty Stratton, Paxton Whitehead as Ronald Gamble in the 1977 production of* **Thark** *by Ben Travers.*

5 *Tony van Bridge leaps to his own defense in the same production*

6 *Scene from* **Press Cuttings**, *one of three comedies in* **War, Women and Other Trivia**, *by Shaw. Carole Shelley as Lady Corinthia and James Valentine as General Mitchener, 1971*

7 *Carole Shelley with Barbara Hamilton as Mrs Banger in another scene from* **Press Cuttings**

1    *The 1980 production of Shaw's* **Misalliance**. *David Dodimead as Lord Summerhays, Peter Hutt as Johnny Tarleton*

2    **Misalliance**, *1966 production, Zoë Caldwell as Lina Szczepanow-ska, Tom Kneebone as Bentley Summerhays*

3    *Also from the 1966 production, Susan Clark as Hypatia Tarleton, Paul Craig as Johnny Tarleton, Tom Kneebone as Bentley Summerhays, Zoë Caldwell as Lina Szczepanow-ska, Leslie Yeo as Mr Tarleton, Betty Leighton as Mrs Tarleton*

4   **Misalliance** *was also produced in 1972. James Valentine as Joseph Percival, Betty Leighton as Mrs Tarleton, Angela Wood as Lina Szczepan-* *owska, Ronald Drake as Mr Tarleton, 'Wenna Shaw as Hypatia Tarleton, Malcolm Armstrong as Johnny Tarleton*

1 *The design by Hilary Corbett of the aviators' costumes for the 1972 production of* **Misalliance**

2 *The actual costumes worn by aviators James Valentine and Angela Wood*

**3**   *Tony van Bridge as Colonel*
*Tallboys and Heath Lamberts as*
*Private Meek in Shaw's* **Too True to**
**be Good,** *1974*

**1**   *Domini Blythe as the Patient,*
*Elizabeth Shepherd as the Night*
*Nurse, Tony van Bridge as Colonel*
*Tallboys in* **Too True to be Good**

**2**   *A tense moment from the same*
*production, Elizabeth Shepherd,*
*Domini Blythe*

3　*Elizabeth Shepherd as Eliza
Doolittle, Stuart Kent as the Bystander and Powys Thomas as Professor
Higgins in the opening scene of
Shaw's* **Pygmalion**, *1975*

4　*Eliza transformed. Elizabeth
Shepherd and Powys Thomas*

**1**  *Tony van Bridge as Alfred Doolittle with Elizabeth Shepherd as Eliza from the 1974 production of* **Pygmalion**

2    *Georges Feydeau's* **A Flea in her
Ear**. *Dana Ivey as Lucienne Home-
nides De Histangua, Christopher
Newton as Camille Chandebise,
1980*

**1**   *Heath Lamberts as  Chandebise,
Jack Medley as Doctor Finache in* **A
Flea in her Ear**

**2**   *Heath Lamberts astonishes the
company in another scene from the
same production*

3    *The 1971 production of* **The Philanderer**. *Louise Marleau as Julia Craven, James Valentine as Dr Paramore, Patricia Collins as Grace Tranfield*

4    *Louise Marleau with Paxton Whitehead as Leonard Charteris in the same production*

**1**    *The most recent production of*
**The Philanderer***, 1980, Christopher
Newton as Leonard Charteris, Susan
Wright as Julia Craven*

**2**    *Paxton Whitehead as Captain
Edstaston, Dana Ivey as Empress
Catherine the Second in Shaw's*
**Great Catherine***, 1977*

3    *Zoë Caldwell as Orinthia and*
*Paxton Whitehead as King Magnus*
*in the show-stopping sprawl scene*
*from* **The Apple Cart***, 1966*

**1**   *Colin Fox as Bernard Shaw, Pat Galloway as Mrs Patrick Campbell in Jerome Kilty's* **Dear Liar***, 1979*

**2**   *From the 1970 production of Shaw's* **Candida***. Stanley Holloway as Burgess, Frances Hyland as Candida*

**3**   *Tony van Bridge as Morell, Frances Hyland as Candida, from the same production*

4    Wensley Pithey as the Earl of
Loam in the 1976 production of **The
Admirable Crichton** by J. M. Barrie

5    Michael Ball as Crichton and
Pamela Brook as Tweeny in the
same production

**1**  *Kate Reid as Rummy Mitchens,*
*Janet Amos as Barbara Undershaft*
*in Shaw's* **Major Barbara**, *1978*

**2**  *Eric House as Drinkwater and*
*Gillie Fenwick as Rankin in the*
*1979 production of Shaw's* **Captain**
**Brassbound's Conversion**

**3**  *From the same production, Pat*
*Galloway as Lady Cicely Waynflete*
*and Peggy Coffey as Muley*

4    *Alan Scarfe as Dick Dudgeon,*
*Domini Blythe as Judith in Shaw's*
**The Devil's Disciple,** *1974*

5    *Dick Dudgeon prepared to*
*hang in the same production. Also*
*in the cast James Valentine, Stuart*
*Kent, Tony van Bridge and Norman*
*Welsh*

6    *Heath Lamberts as Christopher*
*Dudgeon in the touring production*
*in 1975 to celebrate the United*
*States' bi-centennial*

1    *Leslie Yeo as the waiter in*
*Shaw's* **You Never Can Tell**, *1979*

**2**    *The same scene from an earlier (1973) production with Stanley Holloway as William the waiter serving Norman Welsh as Crampton*

**3**    *Norman Welsh again and Paxton Whitehead as Valentine the dentist in the 1973 production*

1   **You Never Can Tell**, *1979, with Merrilyn Gann as Gloria Clandon and Mary Savidge as Mrs Clandon*

2   *The masked ball that unmasks everyone, James Valentine as Bohun, Peter Blais as Harlequin, 'Wenna Shaw as Columbine and Norman Welsh as Crampton*

3

4

3    *Sheila McCarthy and Barbara Barsky in* **Puttin' On the Ritz**, *an original revue from Victoria's Belfry Theatre incorporated in the Shaw Festival's 1980 season*

4    *Claude Tessier dreaming of Sheila McCarthy in a sequence from the same production*

1    *Anton Chekhov's* **The Cherry Orchard**. *Deborah Kipp as Varya, Carole Shelley as Madame Ranevsky, Gillie Fenwick as Firs, 1980*

2    *Noel Coward's* **Tonight at 8:30,** *1971. Carole Shelley as Louise Charteris, Hiram Sherman as Hubert Charteris, Paxton Whitehead as Karl Sandys*

3 *Mary Savidge as Miss Moffat the schoolteacher, Peter Hutt as Morgan in Emlyn Williams'* **The Corn is Green**, *1979*

4 *Peter Hutt with the Welsh miners from the same production*

**1**   *Shaw's* **Arms and the Man**.
*Pamela Brook as Louka, Paxton
Whitehead as Major Sergius
Saranoff, 1976*

**2**   *Tony van Bridge as the Devil in
a 1977 production of* **Man and
Superman**

**3**   *Barry Morse as Don Juan in*
**Man and Superman**, *1966. Also in
the cast Norman Welsh, Hugh Webster and Pat Galloway*

**4**   *Henrik Ibsen's* **John Gabriel
Borkman**, *1978. Douglas Campbell
in the title role*

**5**   *Ian Richardson in the dual role
of Jack Tanner and Don Juan in*
**Man and Superman**, *1977*

**1**   *John Swindells as the Captain of the Guard, Stephen Markle as Mamillius in* **The Brass Butterfly** *by William Golding, 1973*

**2**   *Also from* **The Brass Butterfly**, *James Valentine as the inventor Phanocles with Stephen Markle as Mamillius and Lockwood West as the Emperor*

**4**   *Shaw's* **Caesar and Cleopatra** *1975 with Edward Atienza and Domini Blythe in the title roles*

**3**   *Shaw's* **Back to Methuselah: Part One**, *1969. Frances Hyland as Eve, Jonathan White as Adam*

**5** *The Festival Theatre closely hugging the ground lest it be too intrusive on the town's classical landscape*

1　　*The historic nineteenth-century Court House, first home of the Shaw Festival*

2　　*The classic architecture and generous shade trees are the joint delights of Niagara-on-the-Lake*

3　　*The old apothecary shop in its peaceful setting on the main street, now a museum of pharmacology*

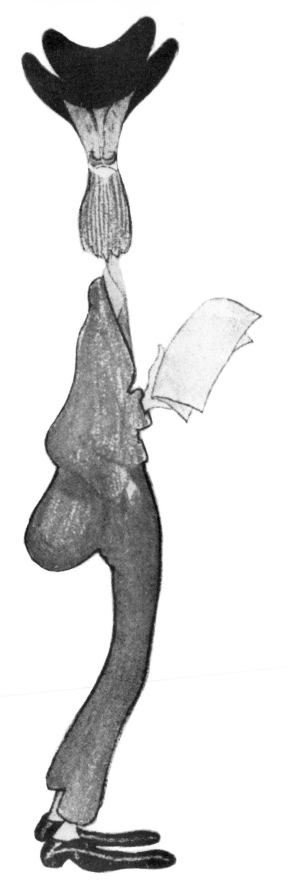

4    *Max Beerbohm's caricature of*
*George Bernard Shaw, in itself a*
*witty comment on the life of GBS*

# The Charlottetown Festival

PRINCE EDWARD ISLAND *is a lovely place. Mile after mile of white-sand beaches; even more miles of red-earth roads that slash straight through the fertile fields of potatoes and grain. The houses are trim, their white paint glistening in the sun; the villages neat. And always on the horizon is the blue, sparkling sea.*

*The pace of life is slow, the people courteous to visitors. It is a family place, and a place best suited for a family holiday.*

*We first went there camping, in 1965. Oh, not genuine camping, with unruly canvas tents and hard-to-find pegs, but with a tent trailer which, when pulled out at either end, flipped up its own canvas to house two ready-made and comfortable double beds. We parked at St. Peter's, a campground by a river, far enough from everywhere yet not too far from anywhere. Lobster suppers were served at a church ten minutes' drive* away, and the Charlottetown Festival was only a few miles further. We had not booked seats for that very first festival but we did know the artistic director, Mavor Moore. "We have come a thousand miles," said I, "to see your show, and cannot get a seat."

"Come ten miles more tonight," said he, "and we will fit you in."

He did. In despite of the local fire marshal, he set five chairs – rather elaborate chairs from the boardroom, I dimly remember – down the aisle, one behind the other. Our youngest, at the age of seven, was enchanted: "It was all just for us," she said, "and we could see better than anybody."

What we saw was the first-ever production of *Anne of Green Gables* with Jamie Ray in the title role, Barbara Hamilton as Aunt Marilla and Peter Mews as Uncle Matthew. Adapted by Don Harron and Norman Campbell from Lucy Maud Montgomery's novel, Anne has everything for a young family: a spunky, freckle-faced Plain Jane who blossoms into the girl the whole town is proud of; a forbidding aunt who mellows into love and an uncle who in his quiet tongue-tied way helps both to achieve their happy endings.

We saw the play at night and, even more wondrous, went to the house of the woman who created it all the next afternoon – a sunny summer afternoon when the flowers in the herbaceous border were radiant with colour, when the house was cool in its old-fashioned interior and the gorgeous Cavendish beach beckoned afterwards for a swim.

We drove home the next day up the St. John valley, down to Rivière du Loup, then westwards along the broad valley of the St. Lawrence. Though they had only heard the song once, the children, mindful that Labour Day was only a week away, sang over and over again their favourite song:

Where did the summer go to
We had such fun
Now we go back to Caesar
And Attila the Hun
I'm sure all this Latin
Will flatten my head:
*Sic transit gloria mundi*
Summertime's dead....
Who wants to put their shoes on?
NOT ME, MY FRIEND.

– the last line, as it was on the stage at Charlottetown, yelled at top volume.

Nor was our family's experience unusual. Thousands of families have done it since, for *Anne of Green Gables* has been presented every summer after that first one, with nine out of ten seats sold for every performance. It has travelled across Canada twice, represented the country at Osaka's World Fair in 1970 and played to ecstatic reviews in London, England. Said Felix Bender of that city's *Evening News*: "If London's heart doesn't embrace this show, the town is in urgent need of a transplant". Said the staid old *Times*: "family musical at its best". Said the *Sunday Times*: "This was an evening when it was good to be alive and in the theatre."

The theatre for which *Anne* was originally written is part of the Confederation Centre of the Arts, Canada's national memorial to the Fathers of Confederation. First mentioned in a brief to the Massey Commission in January 1950, the Confederation

Centre was the original idea of Dr. Frank MacKinnon, then principal of Prince of Wales College. Said he, before that Commission enquiring into the Arts, Letters and Science of this country:

> The happiness and progress of a people depend…on its cultural heritage. Prince Edward Island…cannot continue as a distinct and effective political and economic unit if it ignores its heritage and neglects its culture.

MacKinnon's idea was to build a combination arts centre, library, museum and archives on provincially owned land next to the Confederation Building in Charlottetown. Such a facility would, in his view, appropriately commemorate the Charlottetown meeting of 1864 out of which, three years later, Canada emerged as a confederated country. It took only three years to bring the country into existence – but it took fourteen to create the Charlottetown Confederation Centre.

MacKinnon talked about it endlessly to anyone who would listen. By 1956 he had received permission from the provincial authorities to proceed, and during the summer of 1957 he visited about fifty facilities in England as a guest of the British Arts Council to check his ideas against their realities. By July 1958, he had convinced the Canada Council, although it had no money, but he had also convinced Eric Harvie, one of Calgary's wealthiest and most generous oil men, who had time, money and experience to contribute to the idea.

The idea was very simple: "It should be a practical, usable monument; it should be in Charlottetown where the Fathers [of Confederation] first met; and it should be opened in 1964."

By 1959, a powerful board headed by MacKinnon and Harvie had refined the plans and were looking for $5.6 million to build the Centre. It was agreed that half the money should come from the provincial governments and half from the federal. Providing there was agreement among the provinces, Prime Minister John Diefenbaker promised the federal $2.8 million.

By 1960, all the provinces had agreed. An architectural competition was organized and judged and, when the Queen arrived to open the Centre in October 1964, the people laying the buff carpet went out of the back door as she came up the red carpet in the front. What she found to open was exactly what had been promised to the nation which had subscribed the money: a 1000-seat theatre with modern stage lighting and machinery, a large library and a spacious, beautifully lit art gallery, together with all the ancillary meeting rooms, curatorial spaces and offices necessary for a facility which could serve tourists all summer and the Islanders all year round.

Mavor Moore, who was asked to be the first artistic director, was not only an excellent actor, fine lyricist, good musician and first-rate director. He was also the owner of *Spring Thaw*, a revue which, as its name implies, was mounted and welcomed in March each year in Toronto and environs.

So *Spring Thaw* became one of the shows for the first season; the musical version of *Anne of Green Gables* was commissioned for another and Wayne and Shuster, those internationally famous but nationally committed comedians, were asked to put on their own show for a third. Nathan Cohen, then Canada's leading drama critic, was mightily impressed. He first commented on Mavor Moore's intent:

For planning the program, Mr. Moore took as his mandate the same philosophy which inspired the Centre. It was built as a testimonial to the founding of the country. The festival is an expression of that same faith and patriotism. And, as a result, for the first time in the national experience, a program has been assembled using Canadian performers and strictly Canadian material which is thoroughly professional in production standard and which has received genuine public acceptance....

"Something wonderful," he concluded, "has happened in Charlottetown."

It's still happening. When Alan Lund took over from Mavor Moore as artistic director, original Canadian musical productions continued. In 1971, Earle Birney's novel about World War II, *Turvey*, was adapted for the stage. Though a little unsure in its general direction, *Private Turvey's War* had some hilarious scenes. An assault course danced by the company was breathtaking, and the hospital scenes with compliant nurses and a butch matron were achingly funny. But *Turvey* was written as a spoof of the 1939-45 army: a sort of Canadian *Good Soldier Schweik*. The temper of the times made its producers turn Turvey himself from a permanent member of the awkward squad into a sort of contemporary draft dodger. Turvey was, alas, an idea whose time had gone.

The festival did better with another war theme in 1977. Again conceived and developed by Alan Lund, *The Legend of the Dumbells* tried to re-create the original Dumbells, a concert party of eight soldiers with the necessary vaudeville talent who were pulled out of the trenches at Passchendaele in 1917. Put under the command of Captain Merton Plunkett, a grocer from Orillia, Ontario, their job was to rebuild the morale of those who had endured the blood and filth of trench warfare for too long. A remarkable female impersonator, Ross Hamilton, was the inspiration of the troupe. So well did they do their job that, in 1918 when the war ended, they became a professional group touring Canada and the United States for over ten successful, nostalgic years.

Rich with the tunes we all know – *It's A Long Way to Tipperary*, *Pack Up Your Troubles*, *Roses of Picardy* and *Oh! Oh! Oh! What a Lovely War* – the show was a great crowd pleaser. Doug Chamberlain, one of Canada's great comics, was superb in it; so was David Warrack at the piano – in one scene, he played it by reaching up from underneath, having drunk himself, literally, under the table.

Singing and dancing – sheer musical entertainment – has always been the mainstay of the Charlottetown Festival. There was, for example, *By George!*, an exclamatory confection by Alan Lund from the songs of George Gershwin. As with the World War I songs, the audience knew them all by heart: *Shall We Dance*, *Nice Work If You Can Get It*, *Love Walked In*, *Let's Call the Whole Thing Off*. The second act not only glittered with its own polish, it was mounted in a marvellous stage set of mirrors, illuminated staircases and flashing tinsel. Its finale was *Rhapsody in Blue* begun by Fen Watkin at a spotlighted grand piano, then joined by the orchestra, the whole cast frozen against a blue cyclorama. As the music swelled, the cast were suddenly fully lit, swooped down the staircase and finally danced up a storm which brought audiences to their feet night after night.

*Anne of Green Gables* always; *Sunshine Town*, *Turvey*, *The Legend of the Dumbells*, *By George!* and *Johnny Belinda* have been the shows which have set both the standard and the tone for Charlottetown.

Next to *Anne*, *Johnny Belinda* was for many years the most popular and most-produced show at the Festival. First mounted in 1968, it was repeated in 1969, revived in 1975 and 1976. The story of its appearance is solid Charlottetown. Elmer Harris, a successful American playwright, bought a summer home at Fortune Bridge on the Island in 1909. Forty years later he wrote a play about a deaf-mute girl – perhaps based on stories he had heard – setting it in Souris, a fishing-town on the eastern end of the Island. It was a huge success, running for 320 performances on Broadway, and was then turned into a film. Jane Wyman played the deaf-mute Belinda and won an Oscar for her performance.

Mavor Moore tried for years to negotiate the rights for a musical adaptation of it, succeeding finally in 1967, and himself adapting it for the 1968 season, with musical director John Fenwick writing the score.

In 1980 *Fauntleroy* moved ahead of *Johnny Belinda* in popular acceptance, and even ahead, in its first year, of *Anne* in its sixteenth. By the middle of the season there was not a seat left for the rest of the run, and extra performances were added.

Both *Belinda* and *Fauntleroy* call for remarkable dancing. But then, so do most of the other productions in Charlottetown. And now Canada's most remarkable troupe of dancers, Les Feux Follets, are resident in Charlottetown, as an integral part of the Festival. Like the Festival itself they are a celebration of their native land. They move from Indian and Inuit dance, stately and traditional, to the lively clog dances of the Acadians and the whirlwind tap dances of Quebec. The laying of the railroad across the Prairies follows jigs and hornpipes from the Maritimes. Energy, talent, beauty and spectacle – that's what Feux Follets is made of.

It's also what the Charlottetown Festival is made of. What else could compose a yearly celebration of Canada's diversity, youth and strength?

At the Festival's 15th anniversary in 1979, Mavor Moore, Alan Lund, Norman Campbell and Frank MacKinnon all went back to celebrate their child. They were joined by John Diefenbaker, who had made the original federal commitment of funds, in a series of dinners, parties and working meetings for those who now continue this unusual memorial to the founding of their country.

With what pride MacKinnon, in closing his anniversary address, said:

> I hope Confederation Centre will always be a national memorial paying, as it does now, rich dividends on the original investment of private work and public money, and presenting, as it also does now, the heritage and talent of Canadians in all fields of culture. When I tell you that the technical specifications for the building were based on a lifespan of 1,000 years, you will realize the Centre is just beginning. Long may it flourish!

Long may it flourish, indeed; and may we always have people like Frank MacKinnon to make our Canadian dreams come true – especially when they are realized in such an idyllic place, where the living is so easy and the lobsters so sweet!

# The Charlottetown Festival

1 **Anne of Green Gables** *based on the novel by Lucy Maud Montgomery. A 1980 production. Susan Cuthbert as an exuberant Anne*

1    *Jamie Ray as an earlier Anne (1965) at the school picnic*

2    *From the same 1965 production, Anne apologizes. Maud Whitmore as Mrs Lynde, Peter Mews as Matthew, Barbara Hamilton as Marilla*

3    *Malorie-Ann Spiller as another
Anne is angry when teased about
her red hair and freckles, 1980*

4    *Susan Cuthbert as Anne,
Cleone Duncan as Mrs Lynde,
Elizabeth Mawson as Marilla and
George Merner as Matthew, 1979.
The musical adaptation of* **Anne** of
**Green Gables** *was made by Don
Harron and Norman Campbell*

**1**  *Susan Cuthbert as Anne again in 1980. Jim White as Gilbert Blythe makes fun of her red hair*

2 *Douglas Chamberlain as the Earl of Dorincourt, Wanda Cannon as Mrs Errol in* **Fauntleroy**, *1980*

3 *Cedric Errol as Fauntleroy charms his awesome grandfather, the Earl of Dorincourt, 1980*

4 *Duane Wood as Ceddie with the servants of Dorincourt Castle in the musical number "Refer Them to Me"*

1    *The Fourth of July parade in
the 1980 production of* **Fauntleroy**

2   *Glen Kotyk and Amanda Han-*
*cox as minstrels in a show-stopping*
*dance sequence from* **Fauntleroy**

3   *George Gershwin's* **By George!**,
*1976, with Connie Martin and Rudy*
*Webb*

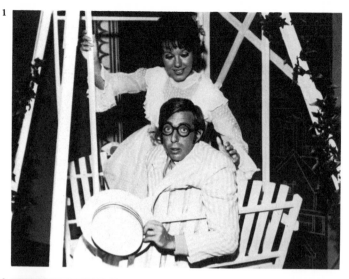

1    *Anne Linden and Dean Regan in* **Sunshine Town**, *a bright and bouncy musical based on Stephen Leacock's* **Sunshine Sketches of a Little Town**

2    *Also from* **Sunshine Town** *(1968), Peter Mews and George Murray*

3    *Jack Northmore, Bill Copeland, Peter Mews and Bill Cole in the same production*

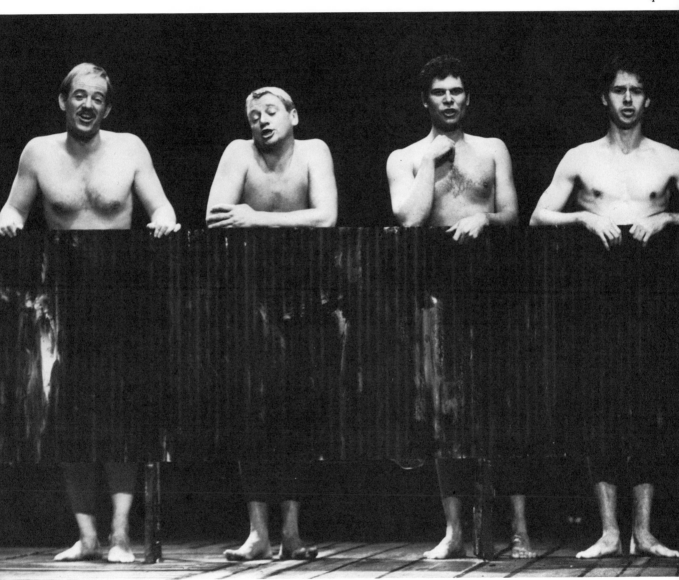

4   *The musical number "Shirts"*
*from* **The Legend of the Dumbells**.
*Scott Walker, Douglas Chamberlain,*
*Gerry Salsberg, Barrie Wood, 1977*

**1** *Jack Duffy and Eric House in* **Turvey** *(1966), a musical adaptation by Don Harron of a novel by Earle Birney*

**2** *Jack Duffy's first day in the army.* **Turvey,** *1966*

**3**  *A hit number from* **The Legend of the Dumbells**, *Alan Lund's adaptation of original material from the World War I revue group*

1    *A lively rock number from* **Kronborg: 1582** *by Cliff Jones, a musical based on Shakespeare's* Hamlet

2    *Les Feux Follets with "The Chicken Dance", a re-creation of a Plains Indian tribal dance*

3    *Les Feux Follets' Valerie Lee and Amanda Hancox with "Oriental Ribbon Dance"*

4

5

6

**4** *Les Feux Follets with another dance that skilfully blends the contemporary and traditional. A dance of the Haida Indians*

**5** *Les Feux Follets performing a French-Canadian folk dance "Les Compagnies"*

**6** *Josh Powell and Gerry Gilbert of Les Feux Follets dancing a lively hornpipe*

**1**    *Marianne Spencer as Jane, Bill Cole as Mr Rochester in the musical version of* **Jane Eyre***, by Hal Shaper, based on Charlotte Brontë's novel*

**2**    *Belinda the deaf-mute, played by Amanda Hancox, is taught sign language by Dr Jack (Bill Hosie). Mavor Moore wrote the book and lyrics*

**3**    *A touching scene from* **Johnny Belinda** *(1968). Diane Nyland as Belinda expresses her feelings toward Bill Cole as Dr Jack*

4    *Confederation Centre is as light
and airy inside as the beaches of
P. E. I. outside. But getting inside the
first time is tricky; not all these steps
lead to a door*

1   *Province House, Charlotte-town, where, as an early Festival revue said, "They sat them down in Charlottetown and made themselves a land"*

2   *The festival of Canadian talent each year in Charlottetown is an even more enduring monument than this memorial to a past war*

3   *Anne of Green Gables' home in Cavendish, P. E. I., is the original setting for the famous Lucy Maud Montgomery series of "Anne" books. The musical based on* **Anne of Green Gables** *sells out every year at the summer festival in Charlotte-town*

**4** *Lobster suppers: the other side of the Charlottetown Festival, and just as professionally served*

**5** *Dogs, kids and picnics by the shore. The kind of summer everyone remembers from childhood, a memory which* **Anne of Green Gables** *renews every year at the Charlottetown Festival*

The fact that it was a lumbering town was strongly apparent to all visitors thither for its first hundred years, since the E. B. Eddy pulp and paper plant regularly sent its cloud of sulphur dioxide into the lower atmosphere. But as Canada became more affluent and more aware of its cultural potential, the Eddy plant was moved and extra parkland was assembled by the National Capital Commission, and by the time Canada arrived at its Centennial there was even enough cultural activity for a group of people to lobby for a National Arts Centre. The group consisted of forty arts organizations associated together as the National Capital Arts Alliance, who commissioned a feasibility study by Dominion Consultants Associates Limited. By October 1963 they were able to present a report which said quite bluntly: "It should be the function of a national capital to give expression not only to the political and economic life of the country, but to its cultural life as well." To realize this aim, the study concluded:

> The fundamental purpose of the National Centre for the Performing Arts must...be to provide facilities which will nurture and encourage growth and excellence in the performing arts and among artists, both in the national capital area and throughout Canada and which will provide a showcase wherein Canadians can enjoy and take pride in our dual cultural attainments.

The site selected was donated to the scheme by the City of Ottawa. Located on Confederation Square opposite the National War Memorial and bordered on the east side by the Rideau Canal, the site had a particular shape which the design architect, Fred Lebensold, transformed into a series of hexagons for the building: one hexagon for a large opera hall with a capacity of 2326 seats, another for a theatre of 969 seats and a third for a studio of 350.

By January 1965 the National Arts Centre was begun, but the original appropriation of money ran out by the time the enormous hole for it was excavated. Fresh appropriations finally brought the whole affair into full and glorious realization by May 31, 1969, when a gala opening week had almost half a million people passing through and witnessing performances by the National Ballet of Canada in the Opera, *Lysistrata* by Le Théâtre du Nouveau Monde in the Theatre, and an English play *Party Day* in the Studio.

Before that grand opening Mario Bernardi had been hired to put together the National Arts Centre Orchestra, a chamber symphony of some fifty players chosen from among the finest performers across the country. By 1971, the National Arts Centre Orchestra had become one of the great musical organizations of Canada, and their travels throughout Canada and the United States had brought prestige beyond the wildest dreams of the Centre's original supporters.

It was now possible to begin the National Festival of opera and music which had been contemplated earlier. By lavish expenditure, excellent planning and the procurement of international opera singers, it quickly became an integral part of the summer festivals of Canada. The very first opera presented was Mozart's *The Marriage of Figaro* with such well-known Canadian opera singers as Claude Corbeil, Allan Monk, Heather Thomson and Judith Forst. Professionally costumed by Suzanne Mess and conducted by Mario Bernardi, it was a hit. It made a trip to Ottawa that summer a very rich experience. Ottawa can be very steamy in the summer, and though the Changing of the Guard on Parliament Hill and a trip on the Rideau Canal by pleasure boat are fine attractions for tourists, *The Marriage of Figaro* in the glittering Opera House was different – it showed a capital with creativity, not just history.

The Opera is acoustically excellent. Its seats, arranged in continental style, are comfortable and the great chandelier in the ceiling makes it a venue which is as exciting as some of the old opera houses in Europe, but with proper sight lines. The ancillary services are infinitely better: the restaurants, the large foyers which encircle the various auditoriums and the changing art displays. It is also blissfully air conditioned.

Building from that one opera in 1971, the National Arts Centre produced *Così fan Tutte*, also by Mozart, in 1972, plus a restaging of the original *Marriage of Figaro*.

Bernardi is a conductor of international stature whose understanding of Mozart and the baroque literature is unequalled in Canada, so that the tempi were right, the playing was crisp and the *mise-en-scène* excellent. But Mozart can be a dull diet, and *Così fan Tutte* has to be one of the sillier plots in opera – all that roaring around the mulberry bush by people in transparent disguise gets tedious. Even the sublime music of Mozart can only save it for a summer visitor if he will close his eyes and just let the music wash over him. So, as the Festival advanced in years and stature, less stylized pieces began to be presented: *La Belle Hélène* by Offenbach was staged in 1973, together with more Mozart, and Rossini's *Le Comte Ory* in 1974.

Italian grand opera arrived in 1975 when *La Traviata* was produced. The production of *La Traviata* was, however, less than grand. The National Arts Centre stage was decorated with one of the worst sets ever wished on that great opera, with Violetta dying in a bed set among crumbling Grecian friezes held together by what appeared to be chicken wire. *La Traviata* can only succeed if Violetta dies convulsively and convincingly. This Violetta seemed to die of revulsion and embarrassment.

Furthermore, the great area of the stage was so cluttered and cramped that the Spanish dance, though brilliantly executed, was done on an area about the size of a pocket handkerchief. Musically, by 1975 Festival Ottawa had come of age, but like Violetta, the staging was dying of conspicuous consumption.

Several reviewers said so, in somewhat caustic press notices. So for 1976 a great revolution came about. In that year the Festival produced a most technologically complicated and incredibly moving performance of Tchaikovsky's *The Queen of Spades*, designed by Josef Svoboda. Svoboda, who was responsible for the outstanding Czech pavilion at Expo '67 and the two mixed-media techniques that took the world by storm there, relies entirely on illusion for his scenic effects. As the programme notes said of him: "Svoboda's hallmark is the innovative use of an array of visual, electrical and mechanical devices in a constant attempt to redefine traditional boundaries of the technical and artistic areas of stage design."

The results were, for *The Queen of Spades*, just as magnificent as they were in a different sense at Expo. The story for which the effects were devised is in its essence simple: a young officer called Hermann has fallen in love with a young girl called Lisa. He is impecunious, however, and she is the ward of a wealthy countess. The only way he can ever hope to have enough money to marry her is to win a huge sum at cards.

Now Lisa's guardian is wealthy because she has the secret of winning at cards and therefore, when Lisa gives Hermann the key to the house so that they may have a romantic assignation, he concentrates on getting the secret from the countess instead of seeking lusher favours from Lisa. The countess tells him her secret – three, seven, ace – and then drops dead of shock from having done so. Lisa, not realizing that her lover wants the code only to win enough money to marry her, feels she has been slighted; her heart broken by Hermann's apparent indifference, she commits suicide by jumping into the river.

Hermann makes a great wager and wins with the three. He then doubles the stakes and wins with the seven. Only the prince has enough money to gamble against him when he doubles the stakes again (and it is even more piquant that the prince is an equally ardent suitor for Lisa). But when the card turns up, it is not the ace, it is the queen of spades. So Hermann, who has lost his love *and* his credibility, commits suicide. Most of the story is told by flashback from the room in the asylum where the paranoid Hermann has been committed. This room was constructed only of insubstantial scrim. On it was projected what appeared to be solid, rough-cast stone. Lisa and her guardian appeared upstage and, with special lighting effects, were clearly visible to the audience as if through the cell wall. Not only was this a startling visual effect, but it also meant that we identified with Hermann and saw the whole opera, as it were, through his obsessed mind.

Not that realism was absent. When Lisa committed suicide, there was a very substantial promenade rail the whole width of the stage and a very solid park bench. When she leaped from the bench, the whole stage picture suddenly became one of swirling water and we, almost as physically as she, felt the river engulfing us. In just the same way our emotions were from time to time totally involved in the swirling of cards – a whole snowstorm of cards all over the stage.

It is one thing to have such remarkable scenic effects so beautifully worked in with the development of character in the opera and to see how the interactions of those characters are resolved in the plot. It is quite another to find operatic singers who can match that involvement with the necessary acting technique, since opera singers on the whole are, by definition, more concerned with voice than action.

But in Jon Vickers, one of the great tenors of the world, Canada also has one of the great operatic actors. As Hermann he was on stage for the whole of the opera, beginning by muttering in his madness, "three, seven, ace", and ending, his wrists slashed by the sharp edge of a broken mirror, dead. Vickers' concentration produced a total immersion in Hermann's paranoia, but his voice did justice to Tchaikovsky. Even when Brian Law had the Arts Centre orchestra going full blast, he could soar above it as if it were not there. The audience on that opening night stood to cheer *The Queen of Spades* and remained standing for something like a dozen curtain calls. As the curtain came down for the last time, the woman sitting next to me, whom I did not know, grabbed my wrist and said, "Wow! I have goose bumps all over me." (She was right, too, because she had on a backless dress, and I checked.)

It was gratifying to think that, technically, such a performance could be mounted at the National Arts Centre. It was equally gratifying that two of the three leads were Canadians of international reputation, and that the whole affair happened on the same night as the opening of the Olympics in Montreal less than a hundred miles away, and yet played to a crowded house. In the audience were quite a group of critics who had come from all across Canada, the U.S. and Europe to attend a three-day seminar in the studio of the National Arts Centre. There were critics from Poland, Romania, Israel and France, and such well-known people as Clive Barnes of the *New York Times*, Edward Greenfield from the *Guardian*, Ronald Bryden (formerly with the *New Statesman*) and Bernard Levin from the *Times* of London. With that production, with these critics in the audience, the National Arts Centre's Festival Ottawa became an international event.

The Festival had hit its stride and from 1977 to 1980 it produced such differing works as Strauss' *Ariadne auf Naxos*, Donizetti's *Don Pasquale* and, still faithful to Mozart, *The Magic Flute*. By now, not only was Lotfi Mansouri coming in from the Canadian Opera Company in Toronto to direct, but the productions were on a two-way street. *The Magic Flute* went off after the summer to the Canadian Opera season in Toronto, and to round out the Ottawa season, the Banff Centre of Fine Arts brought in two one-acters – Menotti's *The Telephone* and Wolf-Ferrari's *The Secret of Susanna*. In 1979 it was no longer possible for any critic worth his salt in Canada, the United States or Europe for that matter, to miss the National Arts Centre's Festival.

In 1979 we left our summer cottage in the Thousand Islands, our faces bronzed by the sun and our hands calloused by the physical work that any cottage needs after the winter, and within an hour or so of stepping off the boat at Kingston's dock, we arrived at the Centre to see a restaging of *The Queen of Spades*. All the paraphernalia by Svoboda had been brought back, but Jon Vickers, who had sung it so well before, was not available. In his stead was Jacque Trussel, a world-class tenor from the New York State Opera. Lilian Sukis, a Canadian soprano who had made her name with the Bavarian State Opera in Munich and with the Vienna State Opera, sang the role of Lisa, and Maureen Forrester, that ornament of Canadian opera stage, was once again magnificent as the old countess.

Under the baton of Franz-Paul Decker, Tchaikovsky's opera came again vividly to life. As Tchaikovsky himself said, "*The Queen of Spades* is truly my masterpiece. Certain scenes fill me with terror, with fear and emotion." So they did us at the National Arts Centre.

The next night, strengthened by a brilliant summer day in Ottawa with a poolside luncheon organized by the staff of the National Arts Centre, we saw the new production of *Cendrillon* (*Cinderella*). Composed by Jules Massenet as entertainment, the opera is as insubstantial as the story itself. The music is pleasant; the orchestration simple without being obvious; the arias demanding for the singers but not memorable for the audience as are Verdi's and Puccini's.

Cinderella must be magical, and the set by Henry Bardon certainly was. An enchanted tree opened to reveal a fairy godmother; a gossamer coach glowed when Cinderella got into it; elves and fairies appeared down chimneys and up rabbit holes – and Cinderella made her striking, pure-white entrance into a truly princely ballroom.

But it was the singing that was most magical of all. Frederica von Stade has a quality in her voice which sends shivers of excitement up and down the spine – pure, rich, beautifully controlled and projected into the auditorium as light as thistledown and as tough as steel. A prince who would marry her for just her feet would be very kinky.

But then Massenet's Prince Charming is kinky. It is a "trousers role" or, to put it in more twentieth-century language, a soprano-in-drag role. So the gorgeous Prince has a soprano voice and, naturally, a woman's walk. Classical opera is full of "trousers roles" –

Hansel in *Hansel & Gretel*, Idamante in *Idomeneo*, Tebaldo in *Don Carlos* and Feodor in *Boris Godunov*. Delia Wallis, who is noted for her "trousers roles", has sung all of these. And how she sings – strong, positive and rich!

For the fairy godmother, Massenet wrote music which soars up and down three octaves, perching on a note only long enough to define it before slipping down or up a fifth. Listening to it is like watching a goldfinch feeding among apple blossoms in the spring. For Ruth Welting's voice, these runs were effortless. And when she and von Stade and Wallis sang together, the texture of sound in the NAC's acoustically superb space was remarkable.

Not all was elegance and air, though. Forrester as stepmother was pure farce, although the voice in the middle of the clowning was still a thriller. And Quilico's sensitive Pandolphe (Cinderella's father) produced one of the most touching, moving scenes of the whole weekend, when he and Cendrillon sat quietly and mused on the whole Prince Charming episode.

Two nights of superb opera. Lavish sets. The remarkable (and expanded) NAC orchestra. The best voices money can buy. Set design, production and direction by the world's best.

The cost? Immense. And for only four performances each of all three operas, a programme beyond the dreams of every other opera company in the country.

Should it be cause for rejoicing in that at least one opera house in Canada sets itself such high standards, or fury because it is done with enough money to wipe out the deficits of all the other opera companies in the country?

Well, all the other opera companies were represented (a conference was called during the July weekend) and no one seemed put out. As one man from Calgary said: "The high I'm on tonight will last me through the lows I may face next season."

Generous, but then we all are generous to the NAC. We are the people who put up the $10 million a year it costs to run it. It needs the $10 million too. For on a previous summer they had done Britten's *A Midsummer Night's Dream* with equally lavish sets, equally outstanding singers and again for only three performances. Ottawa has to have a showcase of what we can do as a nation, and Festival Ottawa does bring a dimension necessary to the otherwise dull provincial atmosphere of a concocted capital.

When the National Arts Centre was first built, there were many critics who thought it would be a white elephant; that we would not have the talent to fill those splendid halls with the right sounds, that they would attract only a small audience. How wrong the critics were! Every seat for these operas is now sold out. The atmosphere is electric and critics come from all over the world to admire. *Opera News* in New York said, "Festival Ottawa...hit true festive standards with a glowing *Midsummer Night's Dream*." The *Times* of London said, "*The Queen of Spades* was tremendously exciting. The opera was well sung in every respect and the conducting of Mario Bernardi...was supple and unusually passionate." The *New York Times* said of Massenet's *Cendrillon*:

> A delightful performance in almost every respect, the evening made one wonder why such a captivating version of the Cinderella tale ever disappeared from view so quickly after its Paris première in 1899.

and *Newsweek* said:

All of the diverse elements of farce and fantasy have been blended magnificently. . . . Even in such a superb cast, Frederica von Stade stood out. . . . It's rare that anyone can make singing seem so natural, so easy, and the sounds so delicate yet sturdy. She and the others were immensely aided by conductor Mario Bernardi – a fairy godfather with his own magic wand. One came away not only inspired by the performance but overjoyed at the renaissance of a work. . . .

In the founding study almost twenty years ago, it had been suggested that the National Arts Centre should not only be a showcase for Canada, but that it "should play official host to artists from other countries".

It has certainly done that.

In looking back at the beginning of the tenth season, Donald MacSween, the director general of the NAC, said:

"Ottawa" is a pejorative in the Canadian vocabulary. Every night, just before retiring, the old practice of family prayer is replaced by the National News. And in the litany of this service, "Ottawa" is used to the same purpose as was "Beelzebub" and "Lucifer" in times less secular.

So the NAC must inevitably attract some of this attitude. As well, it will surprise no one – least of all those of us, some three hundred strong, who work at the Centre – to learn that it is not yet the case that improvement is no longer possible. Even though the level of perform- ance has been high, the greatest success is, as usual, yet to come. And as Canada continues to mature, and the cultural explosion of the last thirty years moves ahead even more rapidly in all regions of Canada, so the NAC will increase its efforts to respond to the hopes of those who saw for it a role of great significance for Canada as the "home" for the performing artists in our country's capital.

Home it has certainly become, and as vicarious members of that national household, we are all the richer for it.

The National
Arts Centre
Festival

1    *Cinderella in a gossamer coach decked in fairy lights. Frederica von Stade in Massenet's seldom-produced* Cendrillon, *1979*

1    Maureen Forrester as Madame de la Haltière in corsets, pantaloons and a dress that has to be lowered over her head. In this hilarious scene from **Cendrillon** she tries desperately to wear the glass slipper

2    The dazzling ball scene. Prince Charming, sung in trousers by Delia Wallis, escorts Cinderella down the great curving staircase

**3**   *Rossini's* **Le Comte Ory**, *a 1976 Festival production. Disguised as nuns, John Brecknock in the title role, Napoleon Bisson as Raimbaud, Claude Corbeil as Le Gouverneur*

**4**   *The opera version by Benjamin Britten of Shakespeare's* **A Midsummer Night's Dream**. *Riki Turofsky as Queen Titania, Forbes Robinson as Bottom turned ass, 1978*

**5**   *From the same production of* **Le Comte Ory**, *Claude Corbeil, John Brecknock and Napoleon Bisson*

1    *Jacque Trussel as Hermann the deranged young officer and Maureen Forrester as the aged countess who takes her revenge from the grave. Tchaikovsky's* **Queen of Spades***, based on a story by Pushkin, 1979*

2    *The spectacular set designed by Josef Svoboda. The ingenious use of projection techniques makes the cell walls seem to vanish as the story is told in flashbacks*

3    *The countess, sung in this 1979 production by Maureen Forrester*

4    *Lilian Sukis as Lisa and Gary Relyea as her lover Prince Yeletsky watched by Jacque Trussel as the demented Hermann*

1    *The rousing casino scene from*
**Queen of Spades**

2    *Brent Ellis as Count Almaviva*
*fêted by the company in Mozart's*
**The Marriage of Figaro**, *1976*

**3**  *Rossini's opera* **The Barber of Seville**, *a 1978 production. Rockwell Blake as Almaviva, Gail Robinson as Rosina, Gimi Beni as Bartolo and Richard Stilwell as Figaro*

**4**  *Claude Corbeil as Don Basilio the roguish singing teacher in the same production*

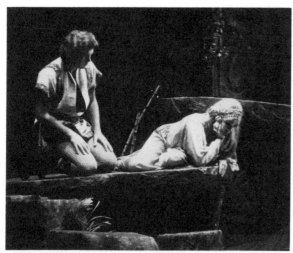

**1**  *Alan Titus as Pelléas, Maria Ewing as Mélisande in Debussy's* **Pelléas et Mélisande,** *1980*

**2**  *Verdi's opera* **La Traviata** *with Louis Quilico as Giorgio Germont and Josephine Barstow as the ill-fated Violetta, 1978*

**3**  *Diana Soviero as Mimi and Neil Shicoff as Rodolfo in Puccini's* **La Bohème,** *1980*

**4**  *Claude Corbeil as Sulpice and Maureen Forrester as the Marquise in the 1980 production of* **La Fille du Régiment** *by Donizetti*

**5**  *Mozart's* **Così fan Tutte**, *a 1979 production. Mary Burgess and Diane Loeb as Fiordiligi and Dorabella whose faithfulness is put to the test by David Rendall and Allan Monk as Ferrando and Guglielmo*

**6**  *Ruth Welting as Maria teasing one of the young men of the regiment in* **La Fille du Régiment**

1    *Young artists Susan Thomle and Murray Stephen Beamish from the Banff School of Fine Arts as Lucy and Ben in Menotti's* **The Telephone**. *1977*

2    *Mario Bernardi conducting the National Arts Centre Orchestra*

**3** *Le Gouverneur's costume for* **Le Comte Ory** *designed by Mark Negin, 1976*

**4** *Titania's costume designed by Michael Stennett for the 1978 production of* **A Midsummer Night's Dream**

**1**   *The National Arts Centre at the heart of the capital. The edge of the Parliament Buildings on the left, Union Station and the hotel Château Laurier on the right*

**2**   *The Rideau Canal runs by the National Arts Centre in Ottawa*

**3** *The intriguing ceiling with acoustic banners of the Opera Hall designed by architect Fred Lebensold*

**4** *The theatre with the thrust stage in position*

**5** *The experimental studio. The hexagonal area in the centre can be raised and the balcony is used by performers and audience alike*

weekend American tourists and during the week was home to many of English Montreal's cultural upper crust. Summer theatre had from time to time flourished there. The best-known of the lot, the Piggery, still did. Why not offer people a real festival, not straw-hat stuff? And since English-speaking drama did not travel easily into Quebec, what with the Péquistes and all, why not offer genuine made-in-Canada theatre at a truly professional level?

In 1970, therefore, Rittenhouse approached the university corporation. In Canada, he said, plays have often been read, put into rehearsal, complained about and, as a rule, found wanting. Yet what was truly lacking was time, energy and vision by professional producers who would doctor new plays, re-mount old, neglected plays and generally give a balanced festival diet of the new, the forgotten and the refurbished.

The corporation listened, pondered – and then agreed. William Davis, a well-known Montreal director, was appointed artistic director. Rittenhouse canvassed support first among interested members of both the permanent and weekend community in the area. He then covered Montreal, especially Bishop's alumni there, and by 1972 had created the St. Francis Theatre Corporation, a non-profit instrument whose initial board of directors committed themselves:

1) to develop and produce existing Canadian plays in a thoroughly professional manner, thereby becoming a showplace for solely the work of Canadian playwrights,
2) to assist thereby in the establishment of a permanent and viable repertoire of Canadian drama, available for production and publication throughout Canada,
3) to make use of Canadian theatre artists, proven and neophyte, in these endeavours, and
4) to create an awareness within the Canadian public of the existence and importance of their own drama.

For nationalists everywhere in Canada this was a clarion call. Stratford, by its very nature, concentrates on Shakespeare and other classical authors, producing Canadian plays only as an adjunct to the rest of the festival. The same with the Shaw Festival. Festival Ottawa, with the best of goodwill, cannot mount just Canadian-composed operas (there are only four). Charlottetown, though committed to Canadian writers, is committed to musical, rather than straight, theatre.

The corporation of Bishop's University saw other advantages. Summer jobs for some fifty students would be created, varying from true apprenticeships in the theatre to ushering, ticket-taking and support staff generally. Festival visitors could use what would otherwise be empty residences as overnight hotels. And small conventions of professional societies might do the same, if the theatre were there as an added amenity.

The idea caught on in the university community. The corporation gave the theatrical facility rent-free. It offered complimentary access to the University's computerized accounting and payroll system. It gave Rittenhouse, Davis and others time from their normal academic routine to plan and execute their ideas. It even gave a substantial cash grant of $20,000 to get the festival going.

Such local support enthused other granting bodies, as well as corporate support from Montreal. The Canada Council, despite all its usual rules against giving to new ventures, contributed a tidy $8000; the department of the Secretary of State, in a separate grant, another $5000; and the town of Lennoxville waived its right to collect amusement tax, which is levied as 10% of gross box-office receipts. Not just because of this latter generous gesture, but certainly with it in mind, Festival Lennoxville planned not only three plays, but also one obvious "entertainment" for its first season. The plays were *The Ottawa Man*, Mavor Moore's adaptation of Gogol's *The Government Inspector*; *Captives of the Faceless Drummer* by George Ryga, an Alberta playwright and *Lulu Street* by Ann Henry. The entertainment was a one-woman show by Mia Anderson, *10 Women, 2 Men, and a Moose*, with all the characters – even the last – played by Miss Anderson.

Running from July 8th to August 19th, 1972, the festival gave 50 performances and drew 10,000 people. It also attracted a great deal of attention from the press: Victor Stanton of Canadian Press said *The Ottawa Man* was an exuberant début for the Festival; Herbert Whittaker, in Toronto's *Globe and Mail*, said *Captives of the Faceless Drummer* was a "sensitive, poetic staging of George Ryga's beautiful [play]". Urjo Kareda of the *Toronto Star* said: "Festival Lennoxville, a sweet crazy scheme, has taken off."

But it was with *Lulu Street*, a play about the Winnipeg General Strike of 1919, that the reputation of the new festival was established. The *Montreal Star*'s critic, Zelda Heller, said of its première: "Last night Festival Lennoxville began to do what we had all hoped it would do. It began to mean what we hoped it would mean."

John Hirsch's direction of the play, she continued, seemed "to be like a declaration of love and faith in the city and the people with whom he began theatre." (Hirsch was co-founder in 1963 of the Manitoba Theatre Centre, the first link in the major provincial theatre network which now covers this country.)

By August 26th the *Gazette*, Montreal's other English newspaper, was able to say: "Festival Lennoxville, devoted exclusively to Canadian plays, has made it. Not only that, it has made it producing the plays in English in a province which is 80% French-speaking, with considerable support from the French-speaking community."

With that first season, the directors were confident that their festival was viable. The audiences and critics were delighted – though not with the same plays. Most critics disliked *The Ottawa Man*, loved *Lulu Street*; the audiences kept coming for *The Ottawa Man*, left *Lulu Street* untenanted.

The university authorities were delighted. A report written for them said, in uncharacteristic language for a report:

> For too many years, apart from a boisterous drunk in mid-October, the University has done little to woo its alumni back into the fold. This year a second attempt at summer homecoming was brought in and over 125 alumni returned from all parts of Ontario, Quebec and the north-eastern states.
>
> To out-of-province alumni, many of whom had not recently been here and who were skeptical of the situation on campus, it was a reassuring return to the place they once knew.
>
> They all stayed in residence, ate in the cafeteria, made merry together and in short, had three memory-filled days.
>
> About 30% of those who came wrote back with suggestions for expanding summer homecoming. And these were from recent graduates as well as pre-1960 people.
>
> As a result of this past summer and the initial attempt in 1972, alumni appear to have a re-born interest in Bishop's. This is more than evidenced in fund giving, attendance at Branch functions and general letters of enquiry.

One success does not a summer festival make, however. The momentum had to be maintained. George Ryga's *Sunrise on Sarah*, newly revised from a Banff Centre workshop production, was chosen to open the second season. Robertson Davies' *A Jig for the Gypsy*, not produced professionally for almost twenty years after its successful production at Toronto's Crest Theatre in 1954, was revived. *Battering Ram* by David Freeman was the third choice. His *Creeps*, a savage though not bitter account of one man's handicapped life, had swept Canadian theatre two years before. Barbara Chilcott, Dana Ivey and Patricia Hamilton were the leading ladies; William Davis, Donald Davis and William Glassco, the directors.

Attendance went up in 1978 by over 10%, and the critical notices were even better. Myron Galloway of the *Montreal Star* said he felt "no compunction in calling *Battering Ram* one of the finest pieces of English theatre we have seen in these parts for many years."

At the end of the second season, Rittenhouse and Davis presented to all their supporters a five-year plan, a plan in which they argued for a lengthening season, the addition of one more major play to the repertory and an increase to seventy-five from the current forty-six performances. They also had elaborate plans for the commissioning of new plays.

Through the winter of 1973-74, Rittenhouse took his plan to anyone who would listen, and to the astonishment of no one, it has in many ways come to fruition.

From Lister Sinclair, perennial of CBC radio, came *The Blood is Strong*; from Ted Allan came *My Sister's Keeper*; from Donald Harron, who wrote the book for the musical *Anne of Green Gables*, came *Adam's Fall* which proved to be the smash hit of the season – and sent total audience figures close to 20,000. Doubling of an audience in three years was eloquent proof of the festival's basic premise.

In the next five seasons, the festival stuck to its last: neglected plays by established writers, like Robertson Davies' *Hunting Stuart*\*; alternated with brand new plays like *Jacob's Wake* by Michael Cook; serious pieces like *Forever Yours, Marie-Lou* by Michel Tremblay alternated with frothy pieces like *Sqrieux-de-Deux* by Betty Lambert. And one musical entertainment a year became common.

In 1975 it was *Jubalay*, a musical revue with emerging star Diane Stapley, which later went across the country. In 1978 it was *18 Wheels* by John Gray, a truckers' musical originally written for the Persephone Theatre in Saskatchewan. In 1979 it was a re-staging of a Charlottetown original revue called *Eight to the Bar*. This again broke new ground in that it was a co-production with Halifax's Neptune Theatre. Such a programme has brought the average attendance at Lennoxville to 20,000 people per summer. It has also given, in eight seasons, over 500 performances of plays by 22 Canadian playwrights, writing about such varying topics as the Winnipeg General Strike, Quebec Separatism, urban alienation, a modern Scottish Faust who sells his soul for victory in a curling match and a prison riot in British Columbia.

The excitement of Lennoxville is not just, however, a flowing of chauvinistic juices. Canadianism of the kind which makes Equity and ACTRA such fools at times is not in itself

---

\*Robertson Davies is the only Canadian playwright to have had works produced at two major Canadian festivals: his *Leaven of Malice* was produced at Shaw in 1977.

entertaining. No – what leads people back to Lennoxville year after year is a combination of four things.

First, there's the chance to see a new play still hot off the author's typewriter. That ensures a built-in excitement since the play may not work, in which case the audience go home disappointed on the one hand, but glowingly confident on the other that they could write something better themselves. And nothing is a better massage for some people's souls than that kind of jejune self-praise.

Second, there is the opportunity to see an old play – that is, a play twenty or thirty years old – refurbished, or even an established play transported. Richard Ouzounian, who became artistic director in 1978 in place of William Davis, rewrote his Vancouver success *British Properties*, transplanting its attitudes and people to what he perceived to be *Westmount*.

Third, it is possible to see all the offerings on any Friday to Sunday weekend at a price equivalent to one Stratford ticket.

But above all it is the ambience of Lennoxville and Bishop's. Quiet rolling country, friendly small town, self-sufficient, Canadian ivy-league university with attractive buildings, spacious walks and unusual amenities. In its proximity to Montreal and its autoroute access, something like a Quebec Glyndebourne.

Can such a concept survive in a province so fierce in contemporary pursuance of its French traditions and culture? David Rittenhouse thinks so. The federal government thinks so. Montreal corporations think so. Twenty thousand theatre-goers think so. Only the provincial government is out of step and starves the festival for grants which they lavish on French theatre.

But then that is a uniquely Canadian 1980's conflict. It is, in the long run, what Festival Lennoxville is all about.

*Festival Lennoxville*

1    **One Tiger to a Hill** *by Sharon Pollock based on an incident in a B.C. penitentiary. Michael Ball as Tommy Paul the rebellious Metis, Michelle Fisk as Dede Walker, 1980*

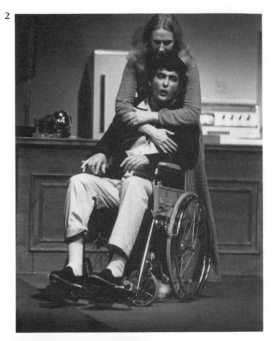

1   *Wendy Creed and Guy Banner-man in a tense scene from* **I'll Be Back For You Before Midnight** *by Peter Colley, 1980*

2   **Battering Ram** *by David Freeman. Chuck Shamata as the handicapped Virgil and Trudy Young as Nora the sympathetic volunteer, 1973*

3   *Brian Paul and Michelle Fisk in the gripping prison takeover scene from* **One Tiger to a Hill**

**4** *Michael Ball and Brian Paul get at each other in* **One Tiger to a Hill**

**5 Captives of the Faceless Drummer** *by George Ryga was one of the plays that opened the Lennoxville Festival in 1972. Donald Davis and Roger Blay*

**1**    *Ted Allan's* **The Secret of the World**, *1976. George Touliatos as Sam Spector, Ron Hastings as Uncle Johnny, Janet Brandt as Marian Spector*

**2**    *Doris Petrie as Mary Mac-Donald and Sandy Webster as her husband Murdoch in* **The Blood is Strong** *by Lister Sinclair, 1974*

**3**    *Robert Haley, Sherman Maness, Miles Potter in* **The Great Wave of Civilization** *by Herschel Hardin, a 1976 production*

**4**  *Lally Cadeau as Brenda, Robert Haley as George in* **Sqrieux-de-Deux** *by Betty Lambert, 1976*

**5**  *Maggie Askey is not sure that eating people is wrong.* **Sqrieux-de-Deux**

**6**  *Another scene from the same production. Lally Cadeau as Brenda, Maggie Askey as Grandma and Robert Owen on high as Nelson*

1 **Adam's Fall** *adapted by Don Harron from von Kleist's comedy* **The Broken Jug** *with Jack Medley and Eric Donkin, 1974*

2 *Robertson Davies'* **A Jig for the Gypsy,** *1973. Mary Pirie as Bronwen, Barbara Chilcott as Benoni*

3 *In another scene from this tale of political chicanery, Ron Hastings as Pugh the photographer*

4 *Another scene from* **Adam's Fall.** *Eric Donkin as the artful invalid Adam, with Bernard Hopkins*

5

6

5   **Hunting Stuart** *by Robertson Davies, 1975. Rita Howell as Lillian Stuart, Roland Hewgill as Dr Homer Shrubsole, Judith Hodgson as Caroline Stuart, R. H. Thomson as Fred Lewis*

6   *Startling news for the Stuart family brought by Dr Shrubsole and Dr Maria Clementina Sobieska, played by Maureen McRae*

1 **Lulu Street**, *1972. The play by Ann Henry that helped establish the Festival's reputation. Ted Follows entertains members of the cast*

2 **The Black Bonspiel of Wullie MacCrimmon** *by W. O. Mitchell, 1980. Guy Bannerman as Macbeth, Peter Stevens as Judas, Brian Paul as Guy Fawkes, Michael Ball as Old Nick*

3 **Jacob's Wake** *by Michael Cook,*
*1980. August Schellenberg as*
*Wayne, Roland Hewgill as Winston,*
*Griffith Brewer as Skipper*

4 *The curling scene at Devil's*
*Rink from* **The Black Bonspiel of**
**Wullie MacCrimmon**

5 *Hugh Webster and Michael Ball*
*up to no good in the same produc-*
*tion*

1    *Michel Tremblay's* **Forever
Yours Marie-Lou** *with Monique Mer-
cure as Marie-Lou, 1977*

**2**   *Bishop's University campus. The
quiet and dignified patron of the
Lennoxville Festival*

*The Banff Festival of the Arts*

THE CAMPUS IN THE CLOUDS – *that's what Donald Cameron called the Banff Summer School of Fine Arts when he founded it in 1933. But it's not always clouds that grace the mountain tops. Often, even in summer, it's snow – sparkling white virgin snow, its edges clear against a deep blue sky as it caps Mount Rundle and Mount Norquay. No festival in Canada has a more dramatic setting.*

*To such a place, tourists flock in their thousands: Japanese by the plane-load; Americans by bus and car; Canadians dragging, like snails, their homes behind them. As you sit on the balcony of Donald Cameron Hall, the town nestles in its parkland below, with the Bow River cutting through it like a silver arrow. To the west, the caravans and trailers roll endlessly westwards on that scenically magnificent road which climbs over the Rockies, through the Selkirks, and will eventually bring* you through the Coastal Range to the flat alluvial plain of British Columbia's lower mainland.

If grandeur can feed the creative mind, here is God's plenty.

So, for years, it proved. Ballet classes, musical theatre, painting, music, opera and a multitude of crafts brought students from all over the continent. But there is no great poetry without great audiences. And there is no real school of the performing arts which does not bring these arts to the public eye.

Hence, in 1970, what is now called the Banff Centre started the Banff Festival of the Arts. Its aims were defined by the new director, David Leighton:

> This festival was conceived with the goal of showing to the artistic world the talent, the energy, the enthusiasm that characterize the teaching programmes of the Banff School of Fine Arts. It is designed to provide at one stroke a showcase for the work of students and faculty, and a sharpening of their skills that can come only through the incentive of public performance.
>
> This is, in the best sense, a student festival. All but a few of the performers are students; the rest are faculty and staff. It reflects our faith in the quality of work being done at the school, and our sincere hope that…the public will find it equally exciting and enjoyable.

Whether it is exciting and enjoyable depends, therefore, on the quality of the students.

In music, those students are all conservatory-trained, many ready for the jump to professional orchestras. In opera, though their training has also been long and rigorous, their voices have still not matured and their stage presence is not yet sure: singing the notes is still a challenge, let alone acting.

In ballet and theatre, the students are less well prepared. This is not to say that theatre is dull at Banff, nor that ballet is a lame duck. With Arnold Spohr, presently artistic director of the Royal Winnipeg Ballet, Betty Farrally, co-founder of the Royal Winnipeg and Earl Kraul, formerly of the National Ballet, as the resident instructors, the quality of the students is high. Also, Les Ballets Jazz de Montréal have, on occasion, been artists-in-residence, and where Les Ballets Jazz de Montréal is, there is always energy, originality and excitement – not to mention beauty.

There is also at Banff a sense of experiment, of choreographers committed to saying something vital and dynamic even within the technical limitations of their student dancers. If such a ballet is danced a good deal lower to the ground than professional ballets are, there is this extra, unmeasurable dimension. Young dancers, though not technically as good as the professionals of the established companies, are often very appealing, their freshness and vitality making up for any other deficiencies.

With opera, too, one can forgive a lot in a singer whose whole being is concentrated on performance. And though one misses the sureness and ringing clarity of a Sutherland or Caballé, one also blessedly misses the staginess and pomposity that often go with the great stars who fly in to "do" an Isolde or Violetta in three days, and then fly off somewhere else to do exactly the same.

The faculty, the other element in Leighton's statement of purpose, is always of great quality. What a delight to see Bryan Balkwill cajoling the right tempi and the right phrasing out of senior students when he normally, at England's Covent Garden, merely has to establish them. Or Mario Bernardi from the National Arts Centre in Ottawa doing the same.

But it is in its musical offerings that Banff has already arrived. Take the occasion in 1974 when Henri Temianka had just created the Canadian Chamber Orchestra – an orchestra composed of specially auditioned youngsters, mostly under 25, who had completed their conservatory training. *Their* purpose at Banff was to get experience in orchestral playing, attract the attention of visiting faculty and orchestra managers and make the jump from trained, talented student to professional symphony musician with a contract signed for the following fall. *His* was to blend them into an ensemble worthy of public hearing.

Temianka was the perfect conductor of such an orchestra. Born in Russia, trained in Paris, Berlin and London, he had been for years the director of the Paganini Quartet, and was then the conductor of the California Chamber Symphony. He is a man of exquisite musicianship, of affable and patient character, yet he cannot and will not tolerate sloppy playing or lack of concentration.

Under such a master-craftsman, whose own violin playing is impeccable, the orchestra made a mainly baroque programme sound sweetly, accurately and hauntingly in the listener's ear: Mozart, Vivaldi and Bach soared out of the Eric Harvie theatre and went winging away down those incomparable valleys. A seventeen-year-old slip of a girl, Carolyn Kirschner, dark and passionate, then attacked with clarity and verve the Khachaturian violin concerto. Her teacher, David Zafer, glowed beside me at the final concert; the audience rose to their feet for youth and talent and dedication as she finished the last crackling notes.

But what else could the orchestra do but play like musicians inspired? Temianka had not only coaxed them and encouraged them; he had, a night or two before, given his own concert which included a Mozart quintet with himself on violin, William Primrose, viola, Tsuyoshi Tsutsumi, cello, Zoltan Szekely, violin, and Ralph Aldrich, viola. Even the tape of that concert, which I listened to a year later in the living room of Neil Armstrong, the director of the festival, made the hairs of the neck prickle with sensuous delight.

In 1976, the music programme was principally dedicated to the work of Aaron Copland – a bi-centennial gesture to a major American talent. Typical of Banff. Not only was his music programmed; Copland came himself to conduct, to teach and to thrill audiences.

On other occasions, Mario Bernardi of the National Arts Centre has conducted, as has Victor Feldbrill, formerly of the Toronto Symphony. The Canadian Brass, a group of five virtuoso brass players from Ontario, have often been artists-in-residence there. Their faculty concert, with an admission price of only five dollars, was a bargain unique to the Banff Festival. And another summer offered a similar bargain, an evening's performance for jazz buffs by clarinetist Phil Nimmons (of Nimmons and Nine).

Music, in fact, rarely strikes a discordant note at Banff, even when it is specially commissioned. One evening we left a spectacular sunset to go in to hear a *concerto grosso* specially commissioned for the Canadian Brass, and written by Malcolm Forsyth, an Edmonton composer. Said the programme notes:

> The work has been strongly influenced by the sense of fun and enjoyment which permeates performances by the Canadian Brass and is couched in terms easily accessible to a broad cross-section of the audience.

On that programme I have written, in scrawly ball-point, "Accessible, yes. Tuneful. Thoroughly enjoyable."

So what does the Banff Festival achieve? A lot. It gives three weeks of enrichment to the lives of those who live in Banff and its adjacent metropolitan centre, Calgary. It creates an added dimension for those tourists in Banff who find themselves suddenly blasted, at a downtown intersection, by a herald's trumpet announcing that night's offering; if they climb the hill to either of the two excellent auditoriums tucked in among the pine trees on Tunnel Mountain, they will likely be bowled over by the experience.

Above all, its pedagogical purpose is achieved. But in such a breathtaking setting, pedagogy fades into insignificance. Mozart operas; de Bournonville ballets; modern plays; Beethoven, Elgar and Copland symphonies and Broadway musicals – all this, and a mountain heaven too.

Keith Ashwell, writing in the *Edmonton Journal* not long ago, said of a play-reading in a Banff church that it was "just another example of the fine arts festival coming down from the mountain to share its business and excitement with the people."

Sharing with the people. Sharing the talent, energy, dynamism and infectious enthusiasm of youth with those who are already sharing the magnificent scenery of the Rockies and the pristine National Park which stretches all the way from Banff to Jasper. Sharing the cultural riches of the world with the scenic riches of Canada. It's a big idea in a big country. And though it's not yet fully realized in all departments, the Banff Summer Festival is well on its nervy, western way, with music nobly in the lead.

The Banff Festival of the Arts

1    *Paul Jolicoeur in* **Scarecrow** *by Percy Mackaye, 1976*

1   *Earle Klein in* **House of Blue
Leaves** *by John Guare, 1979*

2 **Gigi** *by Alan J. Lerner and Frederick Loewe, based on a novel by Colette. Tracy Moore as Gigi, 1977*

3 *Gigi grown up into a stylish cocotte, from the same production*

1   *The young Gigi coached by her aunt in the ways of the world*

2   *Ross Thompson as Petruchio, Wanda Cannon as Kate in* **Kiss Me, Kate** *by Cole Porter, based on the play by Shakespeare,* **The Taming of the Shrew**

3   *Puccini's one-act opera* **Suor Angelica** *presented at the Festival in 1979*

4   *Loretta Easton-Flynn and Don Goodspeed in* **Carousel** *by Rodgers and Hammerstein, 1979*

5   *Laszlo Funtek designed the set for the 1973 production of* **Anne of Green Gables** *by Lucy Maud Montgomery. Frances Ditz as Anne*

6   *A 1975 production of* **Carnival** *by Bob Merrill*

**1** *Debbie Milson and Janet Field as the ugly sisters, with Stephen Valentino as Don Magnifico in the opera* **Cinderella** *by Rossini*

**2** **Rodeo**, *choreographed by Agnes De Mille, presented in 1976*

**3** *Ballet presentation at the Festival, 1977*

4    *Another presentation by dance students from the Banff Centre, 1979*

1

2

**1** **Magic Journey,** *a 1977 ballet jazz presentation*

**2** *Dance instructress Natalia Zolotova with a class, 1979*

3    *The costumes designed by Vera Shubert Lawrence for* **The Good Woman of Setzuan** *by Bertolt Brecht, presented by the 1980 drama class*

4    *Murray Laufer's set design for the 1980 opera presentation* **The Merry Wives of Windsor** *by Otto Nicolai based on Shakespeare's comedy*

**1** *George Gaber and students in a percussion ensemble workshop*

**2** *Henri Temianka with student Alison Dalton rehearsing for a 1979 performance*

**3** *A chamber music ensemble in rehearsal, 1979*

4    *Mount Rundle towers over the Banff Centre, dwarfing the Greek columns of the theatre complex, bottom left*

5    *The Banff Springs Hotel in the Bow River Valley, down from the Banff Centre, where modern arts and Victorian Scottish Gothic now mingle easily all year round*

# Festival Harvest

THERE ARE OTHER FESTIVALS IN CANADA than the ones described in the previous pages. In Whitehorse, capital of the Yukon Territories, there is a re-creation of the Gold Rush days. Gartered bar-girls flash their thighs and tough prospectors have at Robert Service's "nineties" poetry. At the end of the performance, one man is chosen from the audience to remove the head girl's garter. I still have that garter, properly affixed to a certificate of my tenderfoot standing, the whole improbable parchment sealed with a great moist lipstick kiss.

In Gimli, Manitoba, there is a celebration by the Icelandic community there – now the biggest Icelandic jamboree in the world. In Calgary, the Stampede perpetuates the skills of the cowboys who made Alberta rich before ever a trickle of oil was found in that now-wealthy province.

There are craft festivals in all provinces; old-time fiddlers' competitions and festivals in Ontario and Nova Scotia; a *ceilidh* in Cape Breton, that still bleak, still Scottish outcrop of the Eastern shore. There is a Fall Festival in Algoma, when the maples are flaming red and the other festivals are over. There is a Festival of Humour at Orillia, where Stephen Leacock wrote his books on the shores of the aptly-named Brewery Bay, and a Festival of Dance at varying locations organized by the umbrella group of our dancing companies, Dance Canada.

There are blossom festivals and wine festivals; folk festivals (daughters of Mariposa) and ethnic festivals, ranging from Chinese dragons to Caribbean Mardi gras. All are part of the fabric of our increasingly rich Canadian society. All are carefully created, strongly-felt expressions of the cultural diversity which is our heritage.

The summer festivals celebrated in the preceding pages are more than that: they are all of an international, as much as national, character. More, they are all of international artistic quality. A Stratford production can transfer easily to London or New York when the season in Ontario finishes. So can one from Niagara-on-the-Lake or Charlottetown.

For excellence has always been the aim of these festivals. "Nothing but the best for Stratford," said Guthrie, when he first met with the Patterson group there in 1952. "Same here," said Brian Doherty, when he lured Barry Morse and then Paxton Whitehead to Niagara-on-the-Lake. "Make no small plans," said Edward Johnson of Guelph, "for they have no power to excite the minds and hearts of men." And even at Banff, only the very best students are chosen from nation-wide auditions.

In the staging, too, these festivals set the standards for all other theatrical ventures in this country. The costumes and properties at Stratford are good enough to mount as a special exhibition at Gallery Stratford each year. Costume sketches, many now owned by Gallery Stratford through the generosity of Floyd Chalmers, a former president of the Festival, go on regular tours throughout the country.

Economically, too, these festivals bring great benefits to their individual cities. Guelph, through a general awakening of the artistic community there, has built a new civic art gallery. Bishop's University at Lennoxville has a more loyal alumni following than ever before, partly because of the return thither by graduates for joint festival and homecoming weekends.

As for Stratford, eight new industries have located there since the festival started, as well as a whole collection of motels, restaurants, bookshops, boutiques and craft shops. The downtown core has been almost totally rebuilt and the old City Hall has been splendidly refurbished.

Businessmen, whose corporations are constantly asked for money to sustain these festivals' growth, are proud to be associated with them – not just because they bring prestige to their corporate sponsors, but especially because these festivals are themselves big business and control their money well. And budget control has not always been a mark of arts organizations.

Prince Edward Island's tourism has been greatly boosted by the Charlottetown Festival and local church groups and service clubs provide more lobster suppers in a week than used to be served all summer.

There are other advantages: the awareness that we produce artistic events of international consequence in these seven places is shared well beyond either their community or their audience. All Canadians share in these achievements. A successful production of Stratford's *King Lear* at London's Haymarket Theatre is as much a matter for pride as the equestrian team winning an Olympic gold at Mexico City, or Team Canada beating the Russian National Hockey team in Moscow.

International notice, economic lift, community pride and festival spirit: all these things are important. But to the festival-goer they are, nevertheless, secondary. He is only concerned with the excitement and enjoyment of the festival itself.

Summer festivals are compounded of country sights and smells – new-mown hay at the opening of Shaw and Stratford; lilac on the way to Guelph; clean pine and mountain air at Banff. Of picnics under the trees at Niagara-on-the-Lake; of lobsters in the open air at St. Anne's parish in Prince Edward Island. Of superb performances by accomplished actors and singers. Of times which have seen a family grow from excited childhood to critical but appreciative maturity.

For me summer festivals have produced a rich family harvest of remembered pleasures.

I have been reaping that harvest for close to thirty years now. Looking through a trunkful of old programmes and diaries kept on family trips while writing this account has been a poignant, nostalgic but hugely pleasurable experience. It has brought me even more convincedly to the conclusion that if summer festivals did not exist in Canada, we would have to invent them. Thank heavens that, in my lifetime, we triumphantly have.